The Art of Wallace & Gromit

THE CURSE OF THE WERE-RABBIT

The Art of Wallace & Gromit
THE CURSE OF THE WERE-RABBIT

Andy Lane & Paul Simpson

Message from Nick Park & Steve Box
Foreword by Peter Lord

Titan Books

THE ART OF WALLACE & GROMIT: THE CURSE OF THE WERE-RABBIT

Paperback: 1 84576 215 0
Hardback: 1 84576 136 7

Published by Titan Books
A division of Titan Publishing Group Ltd
144 Southwark St, London, SE1 0UP

First edition September 2005
10 9 8 7 6 5 4 3 2 1

Cover and interiors designed by CoolingBrown.

Visit our website: **www.titanbooks.com**
Visit the movie website: **www.wandg.com**

To subscribe to our regular newsletter for up-to-the-minute news, great
offers and competitions, email: titan-news@titanmail.com

Did you enjoy this book?
We love to hear from
our readers.
Please e-mail us at:
readerfeedback@titanmail.com
or write to Reader Feedback at
the above address.

ACKNOWLEDGEMENTS

The authors would like to thank:

David Barraclough and Joanna Boylett, for smoothing the
entire commissioning and editing process;

Angie Last, Helen Neno, Jess Houston, Lee Ferris, Lucy Wendover,
Rachael Carpenter and Yalda Armian at Aardman for making our
time there so productive and relaxed;

Everyone at Aardman and elsewhere who gave up their valuable time
in order to be interviewed for this book.

And finally Helen Grimmett, for her rapid and
accurate transcriptions.

Titan Books would also like to thank Geoff Tibballs for his help in the early stages of
the project; Arthur Brown and Tish Jones for all their hard work; the following people
for giving up their valuable time:

Andrew Bloxham, Andy Brown, Ben Toogood, Bridget Phelan, Charlotte Loughnane,
David Alex-Riddett, David Vinicombe, David McCormick, David Sproxton, Debbie Smith,
Gavin Lines, Greg Perler, Ian Whitlock, Jan Sanger, Jane Kite, Jay Grace, Jeff Cliff, John
Wright, Julian Nott, Loyd Price, Manon Roberts, Matt Perry, Merlin Crossingham, Mick
Hockney, Michael Cooper, Michael Salter, Nancy Jones, Nick Park, Paddy Eason, Penny
Foster, Peter Lord, Phil Lewis, Steve Box, Sue Lipscombe, Tristan Oliver;

And last, but by no means least, film still photographers Luke Smith, Richard Lalng and
Tom Barnes, and artists David Vinicombe, Jan Sanger, Michael Salter, Nick Park, Steve
Box, Sylvia Bennion and Zennor Box, all of who's art work has been used throughout
this book — thank you!

AUTHORS' DEDICATION
To Robbie and Sophie,
for reminding us to be a little less analytical about these things...

CONTENTS

Message from Nick Park & Steve Box

Making this feature film has been an incredibly steep learning curve for us and we would never have reached the summit if it wasn't for all our fellow mountaineers. We couldn't have done it without such an incredibly talented crew.

Nick Park and Steve Box, Directors
July 2005

Opposite: Steve Box and Nick Park with a life size replica of the Anti-pesto van.

Right: Nick Park and Steve Box have sneaky cameos in the film.

Below: Nick Park and Loyd Price (supervising animator) on set.

Bottom left: A Nick Park sketch of the Were-rabbit.

Foreword by Peter Lord

I was lecturing at the National Film and Television School in Beaconsfield over twenty years ago when I was first introduced to a quiet young director who was working on his graduation project. The director was Nick Park, the film was *A Grand Day Out* and Nick's creations, the ludicrously optimistic Wallace and his far-cleverer side-kick Gromit, are now animated National Treasures. Happily, Nick's been working with us at Aardman ever since, and we directed *Chicken Run* together in 2000.

When Wallace and Gromit were ready for their second outing in *The Wrong Trousers*, Nick was joined by Steve Box, another highly talented animator. Now the two of them have joined forces again to direct Britain's favourite smart dog/barmy inventor partnership in their first feature film. I couldn't be happier.

People who watch our films — and love them — sometimes imagine that they're made in a large garden-shed or garage by a handful of passionate enthusiasts. Well they're wrong, of course, but not that wrong. As this book explains, there's nothing small-scale about *The Curse of the Were-rabbit*. Our studio is massive, and packed with sophisticated equipment; but when you get right down to it, yes it is indeed a massive shed. As to the passionate enthusiasts, it's not a handful of them, but hundreds. We're all fiercely proud of the hand-made artisan quality of what we do. Within the studio we have artists, sculptors, engineers, camera-operators, animators, editors — and scores of more highly specialist people. But the great thing is that somehow, with all those people, we still manage to capture some of the simplicity and energy of Nick and Steve's early work.

This book is a celebration of Nick's creations, and of both directors' story-telling skill, but above all I hope it's a celebration of a fantastic team of people who have brought together a whole universe of skills to make a gorgeous — and hilarious — film.

Peter Lord, Producer
June 2005

The Early Adventures:
A Grand Day Out

Opposite: Wallace's greatest invention to date? As drawn by Nick Park.

Right: Gromit peeks through the rocket's porthole.

Below: Wallace on the moon.

Wallace and Gromit's first and, at twenty-three minutes, shortest outing on film was also, ironically, the one that took the longest to animate. It started as a student project for Nick Park's degree course at the National Film and Television School in Sheffield, England, and ended, seven years later, as an award-winning film after Aardman Animations offered Nick a job and helped him to finish it. *A Grand Day Out* had its world television première on Christmas Eve 1990, and it put both Nick Park and Aardman on the animated map.

A Grand Day Out tells the story of how Wallace and Gromit take a trip to the moon to replenish their larder after they discover they're out of cheese. Wallace has to build a rocket in his basement so they can make the trip — all red paint and rivets on the outside, wallpaper and comfy chairs on the inside — and when they arrive they manage to upset a local coin-operated robot whose sole function seems to be to keep the lunar surface clean. The animation is crude, compared to Wallace and Gromit's later outings, but the central relationship is as recognisably dysfunctional as ever, and the film does contain some of the best jokes in the entire series (including the priceless moment where Gromit's drill bit gets caught in a piece of wood and, after a long moment of anticipation, he's spun around and around, ears flailing, while the drill bit remains stationary).

There are a number of elements set up in *A Grand Day Out* which are still obvious, years later, in *The Curse of the Were-rabbit*. The relationship between the gormless, big-eared Wallace and his long-suffering pooch Gromit, who has to rescue his master from all kinds of grief, is almost exactly the same, as is Wallace's position as an eccentric inventor who would quite happily build a space rocket in order to avoid the walk down to the shops. The pair's love of cheese of all kinds provides the underlying motivation for the earlier film and also the means of saving Wallace's life later, in *The Curse of the Were-rabbit*. Wallace's basement is also a key location in both films — it's the place where he builds his rocket in *A Grand Day Out* and also where, in *The Curse of the Were-rabbit*, he keeps the rabbits that he has caught and builds his mind-changing machine.

The Wrong Trousers

Often referred to (by Steven Spielberg, amongst others) as possibly the greatest thirty minutes of animation ever made, *The Wrong Trousers* (first shown on television on Boxing Day 1993) is an almost flawless *tour de force* of stop-motion animation, a film so perfect that you have to stop and remind yourself every so often that these aren't actors, they're just chunks of Plasticine about the size of your hand. And, talking of hands, it is, alas, the last Wallace and Gromit film on which Nick Park actually did any hands-on animating.

Finance is tight at West Wallaby Street, and Wallace decides to take in a lodger. Unfortunately, the first person to apply is a penguin with a bit of an attitude. He takes against Gromit immediately, displacing the dog from his bedroom and replacing him in his master's affections. Having been banished to the yard, Gromit decides to pack his meagre possessions and leave West Wallaby Street.

What neither Gromit nor Wallace have realised is that the penguin is actually master criminal 'Feathers' McGraw. Taking advantage of Wallace's latest invention — a pair of remote controlled techno-trousers — McGraw forces Wallace to take part in an audacious robbery at the local museum. Asleep for most of the robbery, Wallace wakes up to discover that he has unwittingly stolen a massive diamond! The resulting chase on model trains through Wallace's living room and kitchen, with Wallace and Gromit attempting to capture McGraw and retrieve the diamond, is a stunning sequence that not only pushes the boundaries of stop-motion animation — it bulldozes them entirely and annexes the surrounding territory from big-budget Hollywood movies.

It is in *The Wrong Trousers* that we first see Wallace's inventive method of getting up in the morning. His bed tips up and Wallace slides out of it through a trap-door in the floor, actually falling into his trousers before landing in his chair at the breakfast table. Robotic arms come in from the sides to slide his sleeves on his arms and his sleeveless cardigan over his head. This sequence is a forerunner to the similar scene in *The Curse of the Were-rabbit*.

Also making a welcome reappearance in the recent movie after its introduction in *The Wrong Trousers* is West Wallaby Street itself: a solid, brick-built northern street of terraced houses on what appears to be a slight hill. But perhaps the most important thing to have been introduced in *The Wrong Trousers* was Nick Park's co-animator — Steve Box — who now shares directing credit with Nick on *The Curse of the Were-rabbit*.

THE WRONG TROUSERS™

Opposite: Gromit in peril.

Above: Wallace proves he is "liable to be swayed by a penguin".

Left: Nick Park and Peter Sallis record the soundtrack.

A Close Shave

With the immense and unexpected popular success of both *A Grand Day Out* and *The Wrong Trousers*, Wallace and Gromit became a much anticipated part of the British Christmas television schedules. The only problem was that stop-motion animation takes a long time to do properly — and Wallace and Gromit are, almost by definition, about as proper as stop-motion animation gets. Nick Park and the forces of Aardman swung into action immediately, but it was still two years before a new film was shown. And so it was that the thirty-minute short *A Close Shave* got its television première on Christmas Eve 1995 to universal acclaim.

For the first time in a Wallace and Gromit adventure, we have another human being for Wallace to talk to. Wendolene Ramsbottom owns the wool shop in town, and hires Wallace and Gromit (in their guise as Wallace and Gromit's Wash 'n' Go) to clean her windows. The pair have, however, already come into possession of a lost sheep, and Gromit quickly realises that Wendolene and her dog Preston are the masterminds behind a sheep-

smuggling operation. Gromit is framed for the crime, and Wallace has to break him out of jail. Together, they confront Preston and the now captive Wendolene and set things right — as they invariably do.

The Curse of the Were-rabbit unashamedly borrows ideas from its predecessors, and one thing taken from *A Close Shave* is the notion of Wallace and Gromit running a small business based around one of Wallace's inventions: here a device that fires soap suds at a window, in the movie a mechanism for sucking rabbits out of holes. Wendolene was originally meant to be living in a much grander residence — a castle or a manor house — but that was taken out at an early stage of scripting and has now resurfaced as something for Lady Tottington's background. Perhaps the biggest reference, however, is *The Curse of the Were-rabbit*'s opening *homage* — when Wallace and Gromit prepare to head off in their Anti-pesto pest control van — to the scene where they gain access to the window-washing craft and launch themselves into West Wallaby Street (itself an affectionate tribute to Gerry Anderson's TV series *Thunderbirds*). The alert viewer might also have noticed several paintings of vegetables hanging on the walls of 62 West Wallaby Street during *A Close Shave* — an early hint that both Wallace and Gromit have hobbies which will become important later on…

A CLOSE SHAVE

Opposite: Animating Wallace and Gromit at work.

Left: Gromit behind bars.

Below: Wendolene and Wallace face their fate.

Cracking Contraptions

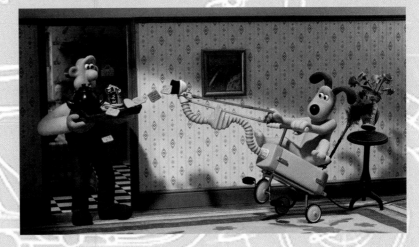

Following *A Close Shave*'s transmission, the most comfortable course of action would have been to churn out a new half-hour Wallace and Gromit film every few years and fill in the rest of the time making adverts. Aardman has, however, never been a company that's settled for comfortable courses of action. The three Wallace and Gromit adventures had garnered them two Academy Awards, one Academy Award nomination and something like seventy other awards over the years, and their sights were set on something higher. Hollywood.

Nick Park, along with Aardman co-founders Dave Sproxton and Peter Lord, spent the next five years developing and making the first of a series of cinematic ventures in conjunction with the Spielberg/Katzenberg/Geffen production company DreamWorks. *Chicken Run* premièred in cinemas in 2000, and (following the abrupt cessation of work on its successor, *The Tortoise and the Hare*) a decision was taken to translate Wallace and Gromit to the big screen. The problem was that few of the team currently at Aardman had any experience of working with the Plasticine pair, and so a project was put together to simultaneously train up new model makers and animators and also whet the public's appetite,

reminding them of what had gone before and raising enthusiasm for what was to come. And so, having been launched on the BBC website a couple of months earlier, around Christmas 2002, *Wallace and Gromit's Cracking Contraptions* was shown by the BBC in ten one-to-two-minute segments.

Each short film was built around a different invention of Wallace's. The Soccamatic was an automated football player. The Snoozatron was a means of getting Wallace to sleep. The Snowmanotron built snowmen. The Autochef and The Turbo Diner both served food without human intervention. The Bully-Proof Vest could knock a burglar clean across a room. The robotic Shopper 13 and 525 Crackervac were capable of heading down to the local cash-and-carry to stock up on cheese and crackers and then hoovering up the crumbs respectively. The Tellyscope replaced a TV remote control with, in typical Wallace fashion, a huge and unwieldy machine. And, last but not least, the Christmas Cardomatic was Wallace's way of producing seasonal cards for all his friends and neighbours.

The ten short films succeeded in their aim. Although they contained little character development or subtext, they got people talking about Wallace and Gromit again. And so, Nick Park, Steve Box and their team began working on what was originally known as *The Great Vegetable Plot*, but would later be retitled *The Curse of the Were-rabbit*...

Wallace enlists Gromit's help
to try out the 525 Crackervac
(opposite), Soccamatic (above)
and Christmas Cardomatic
(left).

PORRIDGE
PROPELLENT
GENERATOR

ACTIVATOR
SWITCH

Early Development Work & Pre-Production

Opposite: Nick Park and Steve Box discuss the storyboards.

Right and below: Various early designs for *The Curse of the Were-rabbit*, including sketches by Nick Park (right).

Getting on for eight years ago there was simply the notion of a were-rabbit as a character. "Nick and I and Bob Baker, who was writing it with us at the beginning" says director Steve Box, "got together and just thought about what story we could build around a were-rabbit. Wondering about what it would eat — which was obviously going to be giant vegetables, if it was a giant rabbit — led to the vegetable competition, and we just started to construct the story around that one idea."

"We had talked about it while we were doing *A Close Shave*," writer Bob Baker recalls. "I was in America in 1998, and Nick would fax me drawings, and I'd fax him back little story ideas."

The story developed slowly, while Nick was working on *Chicken Run* and Bob was progressing his own projects. "'Were-rabbit' was originally an idea for a book," Bob remembers. "That was combined with another story called 'Vegicide'. That was the vegetable story, which originally had Wendolene from *A Close Shave* in

it. She had a garden and Wallace was her gardener. Then it became Lord Wormold who owned the big garden. Wallace was working in the garden and they were creating this gigantic vegetable for the vegetable show because he had to win it. We thought up Anti-pesto in those days, the humane pest control."

Gradually, the story began to evolve from its disparate beginnings and take on some kind of cohesive shape. Of course, in order for it all to make sense, certain things had to be removed or rewritten. "Lady Tottington evolved from Wendolene," Bob points out.

Bob Baker looks back with pride on his time working on *The Curse of the Were-rabbit*. "We were together like a family, Nick, Steve and I," he recalls. "We were working at Nick's house to begin with, and then we went to Aardman's premises at Wetherall Place, where we weren't allowed to be interrupted. It was a hothouse environment for two years."

"Nick and Steve asked Bob to step back," explains development executive Mike Cooper, "and we decided to go with Mark Burton, who was co-writer on *Chicken Run* and who also knew DreamWorks very well."

Throughout the writing process Mike Cooper's role

was essentially to try and keep the script on track. "Nick and Steve's instinct is very much to chase gags," he explains, "and to have fun with characters. It's almost like an embarrassment of riches: there were initially too many things being set up and not fully tracked through and paid off."

Mike was also concerned about the big question: what was the underlying theme of the film? "We weren't looking for a big Hollywood movie in terms of the characters' 'journey', but we were mindful of the fact that it needed to have some kind of emotional shape," he says.

Nick Park, of course, had his own ideas on what the film was about. "It's about Gromit trying to come to terms with his controlling nature over Wallace," he

Above: A Nick Park sketch of Wallace comforting Lady Tottington in an unused scene.

Left: An early Steve Box drawing of the Were-rabbit.

Below: A Nick Park watercolour of Gromit preparing to feed the rabbits.

Above: An early development sketch for Victor and Philip by senior storyboard artist Michael Salter.

Right: Penny Foster (first assistant director) and Sophie Smith (continuity) at the schedule boards.

Opposite: A Michael Salter storyboard of Wallace activating the Mind-Manipulation-O-Matic.

DID YOU SEE?

The Barber shop in the town is called A Close Shave, commemorating an earlier adventure of Wallace and Gromit.

insists. "Wallace represents this force of chaos, Gromit is this force for order."

"Essentially," Mike Cooper explains, "what happens is that Gromit is trying to change Wallace through a 'no-cheese' diet, and that's the catalyst that sets the whole thing in motion and gets them into trouble. By the end there's a notional sense that Gromit's learned a lesson about not necessarily wanting to change people unless they want to be changed."

The next stage was to translate the ideas into a form that could be filmed. With *The Curse of the Were-rabbit*, as with so many other films these days, the key was thousands and thousands of sketches, on small cards, of what Nick and Steve wanted, assembled in rough order — a process known as 'storyboarding'.

"Nick and Steve think very visually," says David Vinicombe, one of the film's two storyboard artists. "When it comes out it's not necessarily in the right order but they know what they want. It's just a case of working out the details to *make* things work."

"We'd worked on these big storyboards for ages," Steve Box explains, "pinning up cards and trying to make story beats to make a rational plot. And then we did our first complete draft film treatment, which was incredibly long and complex. We pitched it to Jeffrey Katzenberg at DreamWorks, who liked it a lot, but I remember him saying, 'Just take some of the cards and put them out of the way. You can always go back to them later.'"

"We've got entire books of storyboards," recalls film editor David McCormick, "reams of them. Those storyboard artists, bless them, in one sequence they drew 2000 odd boards, way back when we first started. You forget all of that. It's only when you go back and see all the old boards, and you think, 'I remember that idea…' Some ideas resurrect themselves a year or two later. It's changing constantly."

Producers David Sproxton and Peter Lord have

DID YOU SEE?

Posters fixed to walls around town advertise movie masterpieces such as *Carrot on a Hot Tin Roof* (a reference to the 1958 movie version of the Tennessee Williams play *Cat on a Hot Tin Roof*).

Above: David Vinicombe and Michael Salter, storyboard artists.

Opposite: Early sketches by Steve Box featuring Hutch and the Were-rabbit.

Below: Phil Lewis, production designer.

borne the brunt of dealing with DreamWorks, who are financing *The Curse of the Were-rabbit*.

"A couple of months ago," David recalls, "Pete and I were out in Los Angeles, and we spent the best part of the day with the DreamWorks creative guys talking about Wallace and Gromit, having seen the movie in the morning. And a whole page of notes comes out of this, some of which we'll act on, some of which we won't. Sometimes, because you're so close to the trees you can't see the wood, and you need a fresh pair of eyes. In fact, at this very moment, we're sorting out the very beginning and the very end, literally the thirty seconds at the beginning and the thirty seconds at the end of the film."

Nick Park in particular mourns some of the things that have been lost along the way. "There are some sequences that I thought were really good," he says, "but weren't necessary in the bigger picture. There was one sequence where Wallace and Gromit set off to do their day's work of pest-controlling, a montage sequence of them skidding around town in their van, saving vegetables from pests. Very *Ghostbusters*, very *Starsky and Hutch*, with them jumping over the van's bonnet, just in time to stop a caterpillar digging its teeth into a tomato by spraying it with one of those spray guns, or just in time to lasso a rabbit. It was a very funny little sequence. But it didn't move the story on."

PROPERTY PROTECTED BY
ANTI-PESTO

THE EVOLUTION OF HUTCH

LAGAMOPHER
WALLACE-US
PAE-
NEANDERTHAL
LEAPER

HUTCHUS
FORMBIUS

HOPPER
ERECTUS

PRIME-EVIL
LEPUR

anti pesto

ANTI PESTO

"There was a whole industrial landscape that never got used. It was gorgeous. But when we've done rooftop scenes and we needed more buildings in the background, we pulled it out of storage and threw it in then."

Andy Brown – Senior set dresser

Left: Andy Symanowski (key animator) and Nick Park on set.

Opposite: A Michael Salter drawing of early versions of Victor and Philip confronting the Were-rabbit.

Setpiece One:
The Anti-pesto Launch Sequence

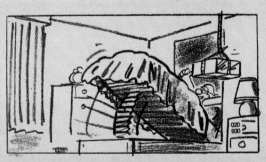

One of the moments that everyone remembers from Wallace and Gromit's previous adventure, *A Close Shave*, is when they prepare to leave the house on their window-washing mission — with Wallace sliding down chutes, being provided with his helmet, mop and bucket by long mechanical arms, and whirling around before dropping onto the seat of his motorcycle. The same sequence occurs at the beginning of *The Curse of the Were-rabbit*, but this time it's bigger and better. The question is, why is it there at all?

"It was partly to start on familiar ground and then expand from there," Nick Park points out. "The idea was: how do we do what we did before, but better? How do we have new ideas, make it a bit more extreme? That was the thinking behind it."

There is, on the one hand, an obvious desire to give the fans of Wallace and Gromit more of what they love. On the other hand, the Aardman production team are very aware that they don't just want to rehash scenes from their previous outings.

"We did think about that for a long time," muses Nick. "There were lots of discussions — do we do the same as *A Close Shave*? We decided that we didn't want to, so what do we do this time? What is the gag?"

In *A Close Shave* it's Wallace who slides down the chutes, gets picked up by long, mechanical arms and plonked into his motorcycle, while Gromit stomps into the garage with bad grace and climbs into the sidecar. In *The Curse of the Were-rabbit* Wallace has been doing some tinkering with the delivery system for the new A35 van. Gromit has his own chute, and the two chums get flung acrobatically through the air together, clinking their mugs of tea as they go.

"This is true," says Nick. "Gromit *is* part of the team now. He does go along with the things that Wallace does."

In fact, the sequence serves several purposes in the film. It provides an instantly recognisable moment for long-time Wallace and Gromit fans, it shows those new members of the audience that Wallace is an inventor and that he will always build something much larger and more complicated than is necessary to do a simple job and, crucially, it also allowed the animators at Aardman to get into the swing of things with something familiar before being thrown into the chaos of were-rabbits and underground chases. And regardless of all that, it's also incredibly good fun — something attested to by the cheers and applause that occurred in any cinema where extracts from the scene were shown as part of the teaser trailer for the film in early 2005.

"A whole naked Wallace falls into frame during the launch sequence — he does have spotty boxers on, though — he's a bit like Action Man in that department. As Wallace's legs went into his costume, we chopped his legs off and had a sculpted costume with bulges in it. It's very quick, there's three or four replacements for the whole thing. All of a sudden he's in his costume, and we animated the full puppet and he falls out of frame. It's a classic cheat of the eye, good stop motion animation stuff."

Merlin Crossingham - Second unit director

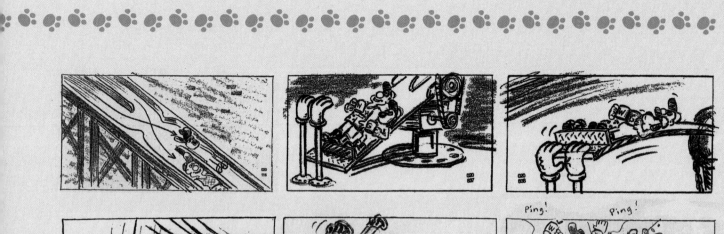

Left: Dug Calder animates the characters.

"We always say it takes place in the cavities. Where the cavities are, and what they are, we don't really know. Between the floorboards, down between the walls? Who knows?"

Phil Lewis - Production designer

"It's classic Wallace, taking the long way round to doing a very short job."

Merlin Crossingham - Second unit director

DID YOU SEE?

The sequence where Wallace and Gromit are delivered to their motorcycle-sidecar combination in *A Close Shave* was an affectionate *homage* to Gerry Anderson's classic puppet series *Thunderbirds*. In *The Curse of the Were-rabbit* the parallels are even more marked, with the eyes of the portraits of Anti-pesto's customers lighting up when Anti-pesto are needed, in the same way that the eyes in the portraits of *Thunderbirds'* International Rescue team did.

The Characters:
Wallace & Gromit

Everything about *The Curse of the Were-rabbit* is bigger and better than any Wallace and Gromit adventure seen before, and that includes a much more extensive cast. In the three earlier films, the only other human was Wallace's lady friend Wendolene, but in *The Curse of the Were-rabbit*, Wallace and Gromit interact with their friends and neighbours, as well as the local aristocracy. And although it might seem as if Wallace and Gromit themselves are the same as they have been in each preceding story, Nick Park notes that there have been quite a few changes along the way. "When I look back at the three films," he muses, "we had developed quite a lot: the shape of their faces and the amount of sophistication in the animation particularly. Now, for this film, I re-addressed them again."

The nature of the story has led to some changes to Wallace's wardrobe as well. "For the first time in a Wallace and Gromit production, we've seen Wallace in different outfits," model production designer Jan Sanger points out.

Wallace has also been constructed slightly differently for certain scenes. The traditional method of making a puppet at Aardman involves creating a metal armature, which bends to hold the puppet in position, and then putting Plasticine around the armature. However, as Jan Sanger explains, for *The Curse of the Were-rabbit*, "it's the first time we've introduced foam into the Plasticine world, and made it look like Plasticine. It's been a creative technical challenge, because it's easy to produce things that are polished and smooth with foam, but we want to keep the feel that everything is handmade out of Plasticine."

Making the models from foam allows the animators to film scenes faster. "When you're sculpting a pair of legs through Plasticine, you have to sculpt *everything*," Jan says. "As well as bending and adjusting the legs, you've got to smooth and readjust the crease in the trousers. With the foam, we set the crease in. We know exactly where it's going to go because the armature causes it via the sculpt. We lock everything in."

To the untrained eye, it's impossible to tell which scenes are done in the traditional way, and which are done with the foam model.

"We've been pretty successful in making that work," Jan says proudly, "using some clever moulding techniques, some dry brushing paintwork, and some top quality foams. We're keeping it in a Plasticine world — there's something that involves the audience so much more when they realise that these characters are living in a 'real' world, they're lit by lights within their world. It's a 'real' world where dollies come to life and teddies jump off the shelf."

"Wallace is pulled by his legs; he does everything feet first, literally. He heads into everything feet first — he has an idea, sees something, and walks over without thinking. Gromit is probably more pulled by his eyes. He notices everything, and goes cautiously in."

Nick Park - Director

Peter Sallis

Although he is best known for his thirty-three year stint as Clegg, the last surviving member of the original trio in *The Last of the Summer Wine*, and as the voice of Wallace, Peter Sallis has had a long and distinguished career in British film and television. His roles in *Doctor Who*, *The Avengers* and *Rumpole of the Bailey*, as well as movies like *The Curse of the Werewolf* and *Taste the Blood of Dracula*, have encompassed a wide range of characters.

Left: A costume design sketch for Wallace

"Wallace is very solid; he has one joint in his waist and it makes him very long and stiff so you can't really do a lot with him. He has got Plasticine arms for some of the close-up shots but we could go into foam for a lot of the shots, just because it's quicker to animate."

Jay Grace - Key animator

DID YOU SEE?

"What's up, dog?" Wallace asks Gromit at one point in the film. It's a variation on Bugs Bunny's catchphrase "What's up, Doc?" – and Bugs Bunny is, of course, a large rabbit...

Above: Some early Nick Park concept sketches for Antipesto and the Were-rabbit.

Left: A final character development model of Wallace.

Opposite: David Alex-Riddett (director of photography) on the Tottington Hall interior set with Wallace.

"Wallace has always needed a bit of top-light and side-light, and quite soft as well — just to define the shapes on him. The biggest problem is the angle. He can look very strange from the side — we try to avoid that because he looks like an old potato and loses his form."

David Alex-Riddett
- Director of photography

**This page and opposite:
Wallace begins to transform.**

"Wallace has been updated; we have used technology that was developed on *Chicken Run*. He was a very basic character in terms of his internal structure before, and we've done some minor tweaks. His face evolves through the previous films — each time, Nick has made small tweaks to Wallace's appearance. This film is no different; we've shortened his head, pushed his ears back — they used to be vertical — moved his mouth up so his head's slightly shorter. He's got a slightly cuter look on this film than the long thin stringy man he used to be."

Merlin Crossingham - Second unit director

"On Gromit, the changes have been much more subtle. The ears have got slightly shorter and fatter so there's a bit more weight to them. We didn't need to change much in Gromit; he still has the same basic insides. There's some technical armature changes in terms of the materials we've used, but he has pretty much stayed the same."

"We developed some replacement on-all-four-legs Gromits for running and walking, just to save time. Instead of sculpting every single step, we can just change the dog part of him — keep the same head and plug it on to the different dog. Then we can replace the dog, and do a minor tweak rather than a major resculpt. He's still made of Plasticine, but we're doing a replacement cycle."

Merlin Crossingham - Second unit director

"You never see Gromit walking on two legs. From the beginning, you've seen him on four legs. We have had him on two legs, but we always have something in front of him, because he looks odd standing on two legs. He's got to be on two legs because he's doing something or leaning on something: pushing a tea trolley."

Nick Park - Director

Left and below: Two Nick Park sketches for the film when the working title was *The Great Vegetable Plot*.

DID YOU SEE?

Tending to his marrow,
Gromit plays it a
recording of Holst's
famous 'Plant Suite'
(more often referred to
as 'The Planet Suite').

"When you're trying to do the Gothic lighting, the underlighting, you have to be very careful with these characters because their features are throwing shadows all over the place. Their eyes are very pronounced. Having eyeballs where you can have a light and a dark side can be a bit odd sometimes, but you have to look at it and decide if it's ridiculous, and move the lights around. There's no great secret, you just sometimes move the lights around until you get it looking right, or soften the lighting because their features won't work with too harsh lighting."

David Alex-Riddett - Director of photography

"One of my favourite sequences is when Gromit goes out to the greenhouse and puts his marrow to bed. It's slow and it's sweet, and there's no dialogue. It's just gentle and emotive. I love it, and no other scene in any other animated film is going to feel like that. It has been an easy target after screenings for people to say it can be shortened, but I am emphatic that it should stay exactly as it is, because it feels just right."

Gregory Perler - **Film editor**

Lady Tottington

"We had a few goes at Lady Tottington, because she was a bit of a problem character [in terms of design]," recalls senior storyboard artist Michael Salter. "The female ones tend to be, for animators. There were a few weird-looking versions of her, but none hit the mark, so Nick took them away and redid her."

"Lady Tottington is based around an original sculpt that Nick did," key animator Jay Grace says. "They literally cast his sculpt, and all her dresses have been based around that same curvy, bell-bottom shape."

"She did take quite a long time once we'd found the final shape," model production designer Jan Sanger adds. "We were pinning down who Lady Tottington was. How much of a stick was she? It's the latitude, to do with her poise, how she presents herself all bent, that gave her a structure."

Lady Tottington is unusual, in that she actually has three legs. "When we were in the development stage, we were trying to work out how she would walk," Jay Grace explains. "She's wearing a dress that goes to the ground, and we weren't sure how that was going to animate. We came up with the idea of putting a third, supporting leg in the middle that you could then magnetise underneath the set, and then use her actual legs to shape the dress, which is just a bell-shaped foam cone. The foam isn't that stiff but it will hold its shape. By stretching the legs out, you can stretch the dress to make it look like fabric."

It was an ingenious solution, but had its own problems. "The third leg has to be on a very smooth surface, otherwise it wiggles around," Jay laughs. "We don't use it very often, and discovered that it was just as easy to animate her walking using tie-downs, fixing her feet down and stretching the dress that way."

Jan considers that both Lady Tottington and Victor only really came to life when they knew who would be voicing the puppets. "That's quite important, knowing who your talent is," she says.

The voice cast are contracted for a number of sessions. "In the first session, you'll explore the character and find out what you want," producer David Sproxton explains. "Nick in particular has the voice in his head. The actors have all these tricks. Helena [Bonham Carter] put some false teeth in for the early sessions just to get the part, and would camp it up to give it the expression it wants."

For some animated films, the voice cast each record their lines separately, but where possible the producers at Aardman prefer to bring the cast together. "Basically, you're doing a radio play," David explains. "When you get them together, you get a much better dynamic because you get a real response, and they want to bounce off each other. A lot of our actors have done radio, and they're more comfortable sitting in a studio doing speaking parts with other people."

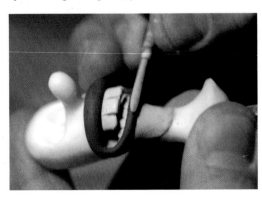

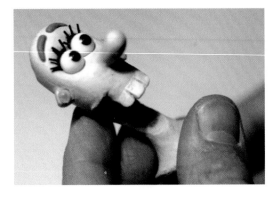

Right: Working on the head for the Lady Tottington puppet.

"Nick and Steve always loved this kind of big red lips, wide-haired design that she's ended up being, but I think most people found her slightly disturbing. The design's very radical for Wallace and Gromit's world."

Jay Grace - Key animator

Helena Bonham Carter

Originally associated with worthy period dramas such as *A Room With a View*, *Maurice* and *Howards End*, Helena Bonham Carter's professional relationship with director Tim Burton has seen her play everything from the chimpanzee An in the remake of *Planet of the Apes* and Mrs Bucket in *Charlie and the Chocolate Factory* to the voice of the titular *Corpse Bride*.

Right: A costume development sketch.

DID YOU SEE?

Wallace's library contains many books, including *Fromage to Eternity*, a cheesy version of the James Jones novel of army life in Hawaii, *From Here to Eternity*.

"When we did the original development of her I'd done quite a sexy walk and it was all based around one particular shot which didn't ever get filmed. Wallace and Gromit had arrived at Tottington Hall and Lady Tottington walks up to them and says, 'Anti-pesto, you're here.' In the original idea, she was going to be silhouetted and almost look like the trees in the back-ground; so you see this kind of big, wide hair and she was going to sexily saunter up to them. I did this sexy, hip-wiggle walk. I actually did that with the test pup-pet and everyone liked it, but then when we came to shoot it, it didn't seem right, and she ends up walking around with a kind of totter now. Almost like a man in drag, I guess. There's one shot where she's on the doorstep with Victor, and Victor walks off with his gun, and she says something like, 'Victor, we can deal with this humanely.' I animated that, and it's a real 'guy in a dress' kind of walk, but it always seems to get a laugh."

Jay Grace - Key animator

Lady Tottington: "You see Victor – there's hope for the vegetables yet."

Victor: "Not the ones I'm looking at."

Victor Quartermaine & Philip

"I think it was always clear that my role in this film would be a lot to do with the new characters, because that gave me the most free rein," director Steve Box recalls. "Wallace and Gromit are Nick's creations, so I always thought that I would make sure that Nick really dealt with them as much as possible."

"Steve was very influential in moving the character designs along," model production designer Jan Sanger notes. "You can't change Wallace and Gromit, but Steve has been an instigating force in pushing those designs along and bringing in the varieties and extremes."

The major new characters are Victor Quartermaine and Lady Tottington, both of whom look very different from Wallace. "What we wanted was like in a lot of British horror films, where there's a backdrop of a stately home," Steve explains. "There's a posh world where something untoward is happening. We wanted them to be stylistically different, so when these characters come onto the screen, it's like they're really posh and sophisticated. And with sophistication came big lips."

Victor went through a number of changes along the way to the screen. "For over two years, he was Lady Tottington's son Tristram," Steve says. "Nick and I both loved the character, and thought he was really funny."

As the script progressed, Victor developed into a more unpleasant character, in contrast to Lady Tottington. "We wanted to have him fairly short with tall hair, and Lady Tottington to be quite tall with very wide hair," Nick Park remembers. "His hair makes up for his shortness in size."

The puppet of Victor was created from foam, which gave key animator Jay Grace opportunities to bring him to life in ways that might not be possible with one of the Plasticine puppets. "Victor has got Plasticine extremities — the hands and the face," Jay points out, "but his body is really easy to move around. It's very tempting to animate him really smoothly and do things that you can't do with Wallace. As an animator, when you get the chance to have a puppet that you can really animate and have fun with, it's tempting to do that. Steve envisaged him as being very stiff, and quite formal and proper, so all that flowing animation sometimes wasn't exactly what he had in mind for the character. You have to find the right line."

Like all the new characters, Victor's appearance began from sketches and drawings by directors Nick Park and Steve Box, which were first visualised by design sculptor Debbie Smith and then worked on by the storyboard artists. "In visual development, you draw many different versions of the characters, and then the director takes it away, and puts his final mark on it," storyboard artist David Vinicombe explains.

Above: An early design for Victor from the time when he was going to be Lady Tottington's son Tristram.

Above: A Steve Box picture of Victor.

"Victor and Lady Tottington are such extremes that it's quite nice doing a shot with them because you've got this devious, nasty, unscrupulous Victor with this totally trusting, lovely nature-ist, Lady Tottington, and so when you're animating the two of them you've got these very different moods that you've really got to stay focused on to make the shots work."

Jay Grace - Key animator

Lady Tottington: "Victor, haven't we agreed — no more thoughtless killing!"

Victor: "Quite right my dear — so I've thought this one through very carefully!"

Victor: "I've spent a long time reeling in that fluffy-headed bunny-lover! And I'm not about to let some puddle-headed peasant poach her from me."

"Victor's legs are designed with a kind of curve at the top, and that curve fits into a bell-shaped body, so you can just swivel his body all the way round if you want to. And his head fits into his torso in the same way, so there's something comical about each bit of his body lagging slightly behind the next. I don't know if that was an intentional animation thing or whether it's just happened, but it's an easy thing to do with Victor. You wouldn't try and do that with Wallace because it would be very difficult. There's been some really nice animation done with him kind of pompously stomping around, and I think that quite often that does happen where his body is going one way and then it swings round afterwards. It just gives him that air of self-confidence and smugness."

Jay Grace - Key animator

"Philip didn't support his own weight properly and wouldn't balance, so we had to have some way of supporting him. In the past we've used nylon wires but they constantly break at the wrong time. We put him on a solid rig which was a lot safer, and we could control it better because it's just like an extension of the armature."

Loyd Price – Supervising animator

Above: An early development model of Philip (left) and the final version.

Opposite: A costume development sketch for Victor.

PC Mackintosh

"PC Mac was designed pretty early on," model production designer Jan Sanger recalls. "I don't think he's changed very much since Debbie Smith first did her sculpt for him. As far as we're concerned, PC Mac's a bit of a hero for us because technically he got us from A to B, and let us learn a new process to put our puppets through a one-part moulding system."

Once the decision had been made to create many of the puppets from foam, the Aardman team had to devise a way to make them quickly and efficiently. With up to thirty units shooting at any one time, multiple copies of each of the lead characters was needed. "The one-part moulding system is an attempt to do away with all seams when we cast the puppets from foam," Jan explains. "You have a seam on the underside where you can pull all the detachable armature out. You then let the skin collapse, and pull that all out through the mould as well. That's probably the most successful in terms of maintaining the Plasticine look."

Since PC Mackintosh, voiced by Peter Kay, is the first character that we meet in the film, it was important that he makes a good entrance, and a lot of time was spent on this. "We did quite a lot of experiments with his walk," key animator Jay Grace remembers. "That sequence is directed by Nick and really it was a matter of acting it through with him, and trying to get into character. A policeman's walk is usually stiff, but Nick didn't want him to look too formal. I think I did six tests before we found a way of walking that we felt summed up his character. He's this pompous official, doing his nightly patrol. He's got a funny kind of Postman Pat walk!"

PC Mackintosh: "If you ask me, this... was arson."
Mr Caliche: "Arson?"
PC Mackintosh: "Aye! Someone 'arson' around..."

The Vicar

One of the staples of the horror films that *Curse of the Were-rabbit* pays homage to is the mad vicar, who has knowledge far beyond that of your average pastor tending his flock from the Book of Common Prayer. "They're always completely right off the map in terms of what they know," Nick Park laughs. "How they know all these things about supernatural powers, I don't know; but they always come out with some mumbo jumbo about 'the beast within us all'."

"When it came to design, we always knew that at some point the Vicar went from being passive and meek, with everything lovely in the garden, to being stark raving crazy when he discovered that the world wasn't such a nice place," model production designer Jan Sanger says. "We were always working with two sculpts for him. He presented a few technical issues, but as a design, he was pretty straightforward really. He was recognisable from pretty early on."

The Vicar's mad hair was the part of the design which did cause some problems. "That was done by just using some flocking," Jan notes, "but you can't just use ordinary flocking material. It had to be made into something solid for us to make it exactly the same for all the multiple puppets."

He was brought to life by former *Are You Being Served?* actor Nicholas Smith. "He's got a wonderfully fruity voice," producer David Sproxton comments. "He also put in false teeth for a couple of his early sessions to make his voice sound different. It's like somebody chewing on something — you get a completely different inflection out of it."

The Vicar incorporates another character who never made it past the drawing board. "We also had a gypsy, who was like a spreader of doom and gloom," Steve Box remembers. "She was called Madam Winnie Baygo, and she popped up selling lucky rabbits feet in one of the scripts. She was going to be the one that spread panic around the town, talking about doom like the character in [the Tim Burton movie] *Edward Scissorhands*. But in the trimming down process she was cut and part of her character went into the Vicar to make him even more crazy!"

Nicholas Smith

Forever remembered as the bumbling Mr Rumbold from the seventies comedy series *Are You Being Served?*, Nicholas Smith spent many years playing villains and henchmen in everything from *Doctor Who* and *The Saint* to the mystical series *Ace of Wands*.

Vicar: "By tampering with nature – forcing vegetables to swell far beyond their natural size, we have brought a terrible judgement upon ourselves."

Hutch

The poor bunny who receives Wallace's brainwaves via the Mind-Manipulation-O-Matic, and is subsequently blamed for being the Were-rabbit, seems to have gone through as many different forms behind the scenes as he does within the film itself.

"He's been a bit of a tyke all the way through this film because the character, in both the writing and in his form, has been transforming throughout the script," model production designer Jan Sanger notes ruefully. "He'll change on set. We know that he's going to go from being an ordinary bunny, but in the meantime what happens can be the whim of what's happening in the script at the time. Quite a bit of what's going on with Hutch has been designed on the studio floor between the animator, the assistant animator and Nick.

"A lot of it was tied down — he had his green jumper, he had his slippers, and he was going to grow — but there are certain scenes where you think, 'Oh does Hutch really do that?' We knew he was going to belch a horrible cheesy belch, because we saw it in the storyboards — but at times he's changed into something that you didn't realise he was going to change into. He's completely Plasticine, so he's not difficult to play around with — which is probably the danger of just being Plasticine as well."

DID YOU SEE?

The voice of Hutch is provided by Peter Sallis — suitably speeded up.

Wallace: "Oh, he may look innocent sir, but left to his own devices this is the ultimate vegetable-destroying machine!"

The Townsfolk

**Right: The Mulches –
happy for once.**

**Below: Original designs
for the children.**

"It's obvious Steve has played a major part in these characters because they're all quite extreme, almost grotesque," model production designer Jan Sanger laughs. "They're probably some of the ugliest puppets I've ever made." No self-respecting horror film would be complete without scenes of the local villagers meeting to discuss the problem, and then rampaging after the beast at the end, intent on murder and mayhem. "We wanted that classic town hall meeting of panic," Steve Box explains.

"We had to have the crowd of villagers having the town hall meeting, a bit like the moment in *Jaws*," Nick Park adds. "What is the community going to do about the problem? Everyone's growing vegetables for the show, so they're all dependent on the ones who are going to save them, who are Wallace and Gromit."

"The characters had to exist, so it was left up to me to create them all," Steve Box continues. "I gathered all the sketches I could find, and we made all these characters. When we were making them, we called them names like Mr High Blood Pressure, or descriptive names like Percival Nice, just to describe their characters. Once they were made, we named them with mainly things to do with vegetables and gardening."

"We built eleven different characters," Jan Sanger says, "which were apparently going to be all the characters we would need, according to the directors. But then they realised that they were going to need more characters, so from those eleven, we designed another thirteen, and then from those we did another twenty-five. We've now got about forty-three crowd characters at various levels of investment of production and investment of design. They're initially crowd characters that are standing behind and doing a bit of moving around. Some of them were made on armatures, so we looked at the most useful armatured characters and then designed from there — Mr Dibber has a pretty straightforward armature design and body, and is quite flexible, so there are four of him. Nobody likes Miss Burroughs as a main character, but as a background character she's great. She's got a good armature, she's really flexible, so her background versions are getting more of the screen time than she is."

"I love the townspeople," Steve Box concludes. "I absolutely adore the film *Local Hero*. I love Bill Forsyth films, and that town hall meeting was my homage to him."

Left: Jo Fenton animates
Mr Dibber in his garden.

Posters attached to walls around town advertise film classics such as *The Loneliness of the Long Distance Runner Bean* (an affectionate homage to the 1962 drama *The Loneliness of the Long Distance Runner*).

The Were-rabbit

"The Were-rabbit was a very time consuming puppet to make," modelmaking team leader Andrew Bloxham explains. "The directors wanted him to look like a bag at times, but also to be muscular and able to stretch out into huge poses, and yet still be like a cute round rabbit." In fact, it took over a year to realise. "I asked to animate the Were-rabbit," key animator Ian Whitlock recalls. "Nick and Steve seemed more than happy for me to develop the Were-rabbit with them, and then work out how to build it."

"It was quite a difficult process to get the armature right," Andrew continues. "We made a few prototypes, which didn't seem to move the way we wanted, so we ended up making an adjustable armature where all the limbs could have their lengths changed with sliding rods, so the animators could experiment with leg lengths for walk cycles and so on."

"We really didn't know what needed to be inside it," Ian agrees. "We ended up making an armature out of wire, and I did various tests with just wire walking along. We then added these doughnut ring shapes around it to give it some sort of form, then the armature was developed slightly more and we added some snip foam to it, the sort you'd get inside a cushion, to bulk it out and give it a bit of shape."

The model makers used snip foam to construct the body, rather than the usual foam latex, because foam latex was too dense and heavy. "If we had made an armature that was able to cope with stretching and compressing the foam latex, it would have been impossible to animate it," Andrew points out.

Even so, because the Were-rabbit is such a big puppet, the armature is still bigger than normal. "The armature is pretty strong and quite difficult to move," Andrew notes, "so we've developed a system that allows the puppet's body to be moved without touching the fur. This is achieved by inserting rods through the back of the puppet and into some large square location holes which are connected to certain parts of the armature. The puppet is then animated with those rods. This means that the back of the puppet has several holes down it for these rods to go, and for rigging points when it's being animating."

Dealing with the Were-rabbit's fur posed a big problem. "When Nick said it should have real fur, I thought he was joking," Ian Whitlock recalls. "But the other thought was adding all the fur onto it with CGI in post-production would have cost a fortune." The difficulty with most fur is that it moves easily. For stop motion, it's essential that everything remains the same between each frame, with the only change being whatever small movement the animator makes. Eventually, they found a fur that had the correct look. "It's super fine fur," Ian explains. "It's on a four-way stretch cloth that has been punched through, and will stretch any way. When you pull most other cloths, they don't go back to their natural form and shape, but this one does."

Above: Ian Whitlock, key animator on the Were-rabbit.

DID YOU SEE?

To ward off the Were-rabbit, the Vicar uses two cucumbers to form a cross, just like Peter Cushing does with two candlesticks in the classic 1958 Hammer horror movie *Dracula* (aka *Horror of Dracula*).

Above: A Nick Park storyboard for a reworked sequence in which Victor and Gromit chase the Were-rabbit.

Right: Ian Whitlock works on a Were-rabbit chase sequence.

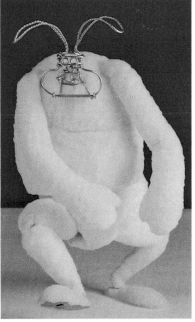

Far left: Ian Whitlock and Merlin Crossingham act out the Were-rabbit's movements for motion capture.

Below: The complicated armature that brings the Were-rabbit to life.

Wallace: "Just a bit of harmless brain alteration, that's all."

"I did look at the original films of *King Kong* and *Mighty Joe Young*, and then I looked at other references like *The Jungle Book*, films with big characters moving around, just to get an idea of how they did it. But it's always better to come up with something original. It's good to view these things and see how they did it, particularly with films like *King Kong*. Performance wise it's great, but technique wise, things have moved on a bit. They couldn't get away with the 'boil' of the fur moving around."

"[Animator] Darren Burgess did most of the shots with Wallace's face transforming and did some lovely clay work with that. There was a shot with the leg expanding, which was a large-scale leg that took about a year to build. I was pretty much there trying to work out with the model makers the best way to get around everything without really using any CGI."

"Nick and Steve were very clear that when the Were-rabbit was running, it would be a different shape, that you wouldn't be able to get a run out of the standing one."

Ian Whitlock - Key animator

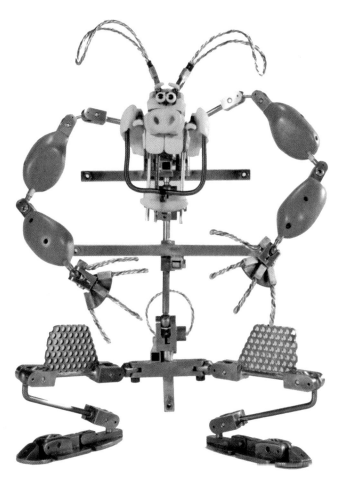

Opposite: A Nick Park print of the Were-rabbit.

Below: An early Steve Box sketch of the Were-rabbit and Victor.

"The head of the Were-rabbit is very different from the other puppets' heads. Normally, the head has the mouth removed and other mouth shapes are put on, but you can't do that with a fur puppet because you'd see the fur boiling all the time. What we had to do was make the whole face animatable. This was very complicated and resulted in us thinking of the head as a separate puppet in itself, made alongside the body and taking a similar amount of time to build. The head has over a hundred separate components, including a mechanism to wind the jaw down and up, and other mechanisms behind the ears which raise and lower the cheeks. He has totally animatable eyebrow paddles, and a beautifully animatable lip made of twisted copper and aluminium wire inside a spring which slides in and out of the cheek, making the lip very expressive."

Andrew Bloxham - **Modelmaking team leader**

DID YOU SEE?

When the Were-rabbit stalks the Vicar in the church, the scene is deliberately reminiscent of a similar one set on the London Underground in John Landis' 1981 movie *An American Werewolf in London.*

Setpiece Two:
Gromit Chases the Were-rabbit

The first major action sequence occurs when Wallace leaves Gromit alone in their van so that he can retrieve the remains of the fake Lady Were-rabbit which they've been using to lure the Were-rabbit out of hiding (the fake rabbit has been knocked from the top of their van when a distracted Wallace drove under a low bridge). The sultry curves and Gromit-inspired wiggles of the Lady Were-rabbit have worked too well, however, and Gromit is shocked when the Anti-pesto van is attacked by the beast.

Gromit gives chase, finally using the car's built-in lasso to capture the creature — only to find that its extraordinary strength is enough to pull the van deep underground when the Were-rabbit attempts to burrow to safety beneath the local allotments.

The sequence required a range of techniques — atmospheric lighting, detailed set design, subtle animation of Gromit, conveying his initial irritation and nervousness at being left alone, as well as his determination to catch the Were-rabbit. It also features what may be the first ever attempt at stop-motion animation in what is meant to be an underground set, with dirt flying everywhere and the only obvious sources of light being the van's headlights.

Building the tunnel actually proved to be quite a challenge, as senior set dresser Andy Brown explains: "I was doing it right from scratch, so I had to develop it as well as decorate it. I quite like doing things like that — you have to think on your feet."

The main problem was that the tunnel had no obvious 'outside' where the camera or the lights could be placed, which required a rather creative approach to set construction. "To achieve the construction of various tunnels that could be animated, I would pull back the grass from the set, cut in a channel and drop in small hanging bridges," says Andy Brown. "Once the bridges were in place I would put Lycra over the top of them, then some brown foam which is scuffed up to look like soil and then replace the grass. It was a simple way of resolving the problem successfully."

"This was Nick's sequence — Gromit encounters the beast — and we all worked on it at different stages. There were a lot more gags in it to begin with that were holding up the action and they worked out that the only gags that worked were quick ones, like the 'Dry Loam' control on the van's dashboard."

Michael Salter - **Senior storyboard artist**

Left: Animator Fabrice Joubert preparing Gromit.

"Nick wanted to have Gromit knitting and play that really suspenseful moment in front of the tunnel before the beast bursts out of the shop — that real sense of suspense that you get in a monster movie. When the carrot hits the bonnet, it jolts you, it really jolts you. But we battled with DreamWorks: they had a slight anxiety over making things too scary, and excluding the younger members of the audience."

Mike Cooper - Development executive

"A lot of that scene was actually lit by the lights in the car. We do have the advantage of being able to use very long exposures in this film. We normally work at a half or quarter of a second, as opposed to live action at a fiftieth of a second, but I've used six second exposures for the candle lit stuff and four second exposures with very low light levels in other scenes. It's a hell of a difference."

David Alex-Riddett
- Director of photography

Left: Sophie Brown and Jean-Philippe Vine (assistant animator) dress the West Wallaby Street back gardens.

The Sets:
West Wallaby Street & The Town

As 221b Baker Street is to Sherlock Holmes and Doctor Watson, so 62 West Wallaby Street is to Wallace and Gromit. It's their home, their refuge, their base of operations. It's where they start their adventures from, and it's where they end up again afterwards. Penguins and sheep can come and go, but the two of them will always end up together in West Wallaby Street with a cup of tea and some cheese and crackers.

"West Wallaby Street was established initially by Nick, back in his student days," says production designer Phil Lewis. "In *The Wrong Trousers* it started to come into itself. We've worked with the elements that were best and strongest from *The Wrong Trousers* for this film. It did change a bit in *A Close Shave*, but where it changed it wasn't necessarily better — where it *was* better we've used the changes, but I liked a lot of the *Wrong Trousers* set sizes.

"It's as big as it need be, and there's no strict geography in Wallace and Gromit's world," he explains. "If we want the staircase to go round the other way, or the doors to open the other way or to move somewhere else, we do it. We have a few rules to make sure it all makes some kind of sense but it doesn't *have* to.

We almost purposely sometimes avoid being too strict, because it gives us the option to mess about with it."

62 West Wallaby Street consists of a number of separate sets, all of which are meant to be part of the same house. Inside the house there's the living room, where Wallace and Gromit while away their days waiting for urgent Anti-pesto tasks to come in; the kitchen, scene of so many breakfasts ruined by Wallace's inventions; Wallace's bedroom, with its pivoting bed and trapdoor in the floor; Gromit's bedroom, with its bone wallpaper; the upstairs and downstairs halls; the stairs themselves, the garage where the Anti-pesto van is kept… and, of course, the basement, where once Wallace built a rocket but now he keeps rabbits. Outside the house there's the front garden, with its swivelling garden gnome, and the back garden, where Gromit keeps his prize marrow in a greenhouse.

Designing, building, dressing and storing all of those sets, and the many others that the movie requires, is a complicated business. The sets are designed within Aardman, then farmed out to the oddly named external company Cod Steaks for basic construction. Once they've been put together, they are brought to Aardman so that the all-important details can be added.

"I don't know how many hundreds of sets we've built," Phil Lewis admits. "There are forty-odd people down at the Cod Steaks building and twenty people here just set dressing. The key crew in the art department are particularly good at getting information out to that many people, and I do have to rely on them a lot. It's very satisfying when it comes together; sometimes you see things that you might not have done yourself, but that's not to say there's anything wrong with that, it's just a slightly different opinion."

DID YOU SEE?

Posters attached to walls around town advertise such cinematic gems as *Spartichoke* (a reference to Stanley Kubrick's 1960 classic *Spartacus*).

Left: A Steve Box watercolour of the back gardens of West Wallaby Street and beyond.

Below: Willy Marshall operates the motion control camera.

Main: The intricately detailed street set – note the poster for Bean Martin.

Above: At work on the street set: senior electrician John Truckle (left); lighting cameraman Jeremy Hogg (centre); set dresser Sophie Brown (right).

"I remember at the start they said they wanted the street quite rustic: they didn't want it over-engineered, but quite cute and charming. It is still far more engineered than it was originally. Not as much cardboard and sandpaper stuck on for bricks."

Andy Brown - Senior set dresser

"I have had in my head the landscape, the sort of place it is. It's where I lived when I was young, around Lancashire, Preston: that kind of area."

Nick Park - Director

"We've never seen the town quite like that before. It's still nevertheless a northern town, and still terraced houses. Still very ordinary working class. There's terrace, there's semis; we tend to keep it largely in the 1950s. We don't have a strict rule on that; anything that works nicely from a previous era is included, and anything that isn't necessary or will suit a good gag from a more recent era, that can be included. But if there's brick, it's redbrick; if it's stonework, we try to keep it more like a northern limestone rather than anything too southern. If there are factories and mills, they've got tall chimneys, and they're red brick. It's not a million miles from where Nick came from, Preston in Lancashire."

Phil Lewis - Production designer

"To achieve the moist look of morning dew on brick-work, fences and roads we used a combination of acrylic glazes. You get a matt one or a gloss one — we do a 50/50 and mix them together to get a satiny finish. We glazed the whole road, and we darkened the tops and bottoms of fences, so that the whole thing has got a very damp feel."

Andy Brown - Senior set dresser

"What I find with Wallace and Gromit's world, because it's slightly cartoony and a caricature of a realistic world, is that the first things that come to mind, the qualities of a stately home or a church or a garden, those areas are the main characteristics. I look for 1950s-ish reference that might help the design along via a book, or perhaps by looking for it for real. Maybe the best time is in the evening when the shadows are falling. It's the accumulation of all sorts of input."

Phil Lewis - Production designer

Left: Wendy Griffiths (assistant animator) poses Gromit for a still.

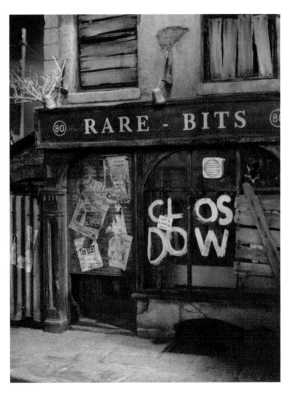

"Sets are distressed with acrylic paints on the whole. You take a plant spray, water the paint down and spray it on, or just have some paint on your pallet, put it on liberally and then spray it off so it runs quite naturally into the cracks. I find doing things naturally is a lot better than trying to labour it, especially for buildings and landscapes."

Andy Brown - Senior set dresser

DID YOU SEE?

The town's antiques shop is called Rare - Bits — a 'rarebit' is another term for cheese on toast.

"Lights are especially a problem when you've got an enclosed set, where you see the ceiling and sets of walls — you have to start devising how you get stuff in there. Sometimes you do it with practical light sources: we actually make light sources that will illuminate the set and look like they're to Wallace and Gromit's scale. That becomes part of the design process as well as a lighting solution."

David Alex-Riddett

- Director of photography

Above: Will Becher animates Wallace in the basement.

Right: Teresa Drilling (key animator) prepares Gromit for a shot.

Opposite above: Craig Atkinson rigging a shot in the kitchen.

"We approached the West Wallaby Street interiors in exactly the same way [as we would in a live-action film] — we want to create that world, we want to make it real, we want to believe it. There's no excuse that it's just puppets — it's a real world, and we have to make it look effective. I think the difference now, since *A Close Shave*, is that we've worked on it for longer, and there's a bit more time on this production. We can research different techniques, but when you come down to the bare roots, I think it's exactly the same."

David Alex-Riddett
- Director of photography

Tottington Hall

Although the movie has many other sets, Tottington Hall is the only one to match 62 West Wallaby Street in terms of complexity. As well as the Hall's exterior — which exists in the film both as a long shot of the entire building and close-ups of elements such as the main door — there are also interiors. Not only that, but there's a conservatory located on the roof which looks strangely like the lair of some fiendish Bond villain.

"It was never supposed to be that much of a stately home," says production designer Phil Lewis, "but it was always meant to be much bigger than a manor house. It was always going to be something that the family had lived in for generations. It was pretty much based on Montacute House, down in Somerset. That is somewhere between a big Elizabethan manor house and a small stately home; it's a caricature of that that grows and develops as much as is needed. You can certainly recognise that it's based on it from the outside view, but the interiors are taken from a slightly cartoony version of anything that suits Lady Tottington, really. A little more extravagant."

All of the sets in *The Curse of the Were-rabbit* are built elsewhere and then delivered to Aardman in a complete but bare state. In order to get them into a condition where they can be used for filming, they have to be 'dressed' — eg bushes, trees and grass have to be introduced to exterior sets and small nick-nacks and soft furnishings have to be placed around the interior ones. Not surprisingly, considering the plot, the largest number of things made for dressing sets in this movie turned out to be vegetables. Not only is Lady Tottington growing some very impressive vegetables in her conservatory, but the town's vegetable competition is held in the grounds of Tottington Hall.

"There's a cartoon quality to them," set dresser Mick Hockney points out. "However, we still researched images of all the vegetables; we have a library of vegetable books. From those, Andy Brown made a start, and then we worked in tandem for a while, trying to achieve the look that Nick and Steve wanted. After about six weeks, we had the look you see in the film."

For something so small and so generic, a lot of effort is put into getting the vegetables looking right. A 'master' vegetable is sculpted in Plasticine and, once it gets approved, a silicone mould is made from it which allows the sculpt to be reproduced many times. A polyurethane resin called Fastcast is then poured into the mould. After this has hardened the vegetable is removed, sanded, painted and, where necessary, given a wash of acrylic paint to simulate mud. Having said that, some of the vegetables on show in and around Tottington Hall are rather closer to the real thing.

"For the cauliflowers, we got real caulis, snapped off little bits and made moulds from those," senior set dresser Andy Brown explains, "so you got the little florets scaled down. There's no point sculpting that. That's what the natural thing does."

Left: The Cod Steaks team construct a model of Tottington Hall.

FOR F.S. FIREPLACE
DETAILS

SEE DRG. Nº: INT/19/06
FOR F.S. DETAILS

250

RAD. 110

5 mm JOG
BACK

VEGETABLE
CARVING IN
RELIEF

ALCOVE

220

265

200

90

75
20
75
20
75
20
75

115

(C)

FINISH AS CLEAN SANDSTONE

ELEVATION DD

NOTE:
FINISH ALL PICTURE RAILS: FARROW & BALL
"PALE POWDER", Nº 204 & FLOSS OVER
WITH GOLD TO ACCENTUATE MOULDING

GTON HALL

92 The Sets

50

40

Far left: Some of Lady
Tottington's ancestors.

"With the interiors that we see, the drawing room wasn't
massive — four foot six inches wide and less than three
foot deep. Most of our room interiors are that sort of
size. It's a question of making the characters and the
furniture the size that they need to be and then to still
be able to get a camera in there."

Phil Lewis - Production designer

DID YOU SEE?

The Latin motto of the Tottington family translates roughly as 'Manure Liberates Us All' (it was originally meant to be 'Free Manure For Everyone', but graphic designer Gavin Lines' translation was a bit off...).

"All the façades arrive from Cod Steaks finished and made up, but they are all quite clean. Our job is to install curtains, put up ivy and moss, and bed gravel around Tottington Hall's driveway."

Andy Brown - Senior set dresser

Opposite bottom: The Tottington coat-of-arms.

"The conservatory went through various phases in the script; it was on the ground at one time, adjacent to the building. It works well with a lift up into it."

Phil Lewis - Production designer

The Fairground

The climax of the film takes place in a typical English fairground which has been assembled to celebrate the town's annual vegetable competition. Each set in the film has provided the model makers with particular challenges. The woodland set had the model makers attempting to replicate something natural, whereas the church and Tottington Hall sets had them trying to represent old stonework. The fairground, by contrast, was all funfair rides, try-your-skill games and marquees — in fact, the same mixture of machinery, tarpaulin and muddy grass that you get at any real fairground.

"One of the pleasures of working on a job like this was to tackle the fairground," says production designer Phil Lewis. "It's just such a nice thing to look at, to design and to research. Everything we do is handcrafted, and to take something that is beautifully handcrafted originally and hand painted, like a fairground, and then to make it again as a model in the Wallace and Gromit style just makes it lovely."

The fairground is, of course, located in the grounds of Tottington Hall, and it was important for the film's structure that the relationship between the two was kept clear.

"There's one unit which is filming the fairground as seen from Tottington Hall, as seen down the lawn," says Phil Lewis. "That's particularly good, I think. It's a set that would have been nice to have put in first, and built, and then we could have based a lot of our other fairground sets around it just to make life easier. We tend to end up doing things in the order that storyboards end up coming out and in which the script is completed, rather than the order that is ideal from our point of view."

A lot of the elements of the funfair — the machinery, the marquees and so on — had to look as if they were old and well used. For that, the model makers at Aardman use a variety of techniques.

"I use Zebo grate polish," admits prop maker supervisor Jane Kite. "That's quite good for making things look oily, but it can come off so you have to varnish over the top of it. Or I've got a dirt paint mix that I use which is black and browns and sometimes, if it's something organic, we'll put a bit of green in and just put washes of paint over it, and then rub it back and rub it around… You just handle it in a way that it would be handled and think about where the dirt would collect, and where it would get shiny."

At the centre of the fairground is the marquee hosting the annual vegetable competition. Piles of vegetables sit on tables, waiting to be judged, and despite the fact that they've been made out of acrylic resin, they have to look as if they've just been pulled from the ground. That's where the skill of the set dressers comes to the fore.

"If we want some mud on a largish carrot, we'll mix sawdust in with acrylic paint and some PVA [glue], a drop of water and you've got a crumble you can apply to the vegetable. And that," says set dresser Mick Hockney, "gives you perfect earth as seen through the camera."

Above: Set dresser Rachel Bowen at work on Tottington Hall.

Opposite: Tandie Langton (assistant animator) at the Giant Vegetable Competition (top); animator Darren Burgess poses Lady Tottington.

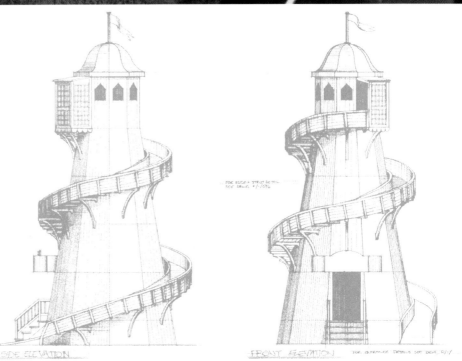

"There are about 15,000 working bulbs on the parts that make up the fairground sets. Visually we know where we want them, but we liaise with the electricians, the sparks, who expect to be wiring up and supplying the bulbs. They've got suitable bulbs and suitable bulb-holders and they tell us what they require. We then work out ways of making them look good if they're seen in close-up, which means making little glass covers and little bulb holder things. If that's not necessary, because we expect them to be further from camera, we have to provide ways that they can be used so the wires are hidden. If they're even further from camera, we don't even worry about that because we know the wires aren't going to be seen. We negotiate that and work it out, and make sure the holes are drilled and predrilled. Arrangements are made to make sure that the prop is the way we expect it to be and it comes back to us for filming early enough to allow the two or three days that are necessary for the sparks to run their bits. They get set drawings in advance so they make the looms up in advance so they can pop them in as quickly as necessary when it comes in."

Phil Lewis - Production designer

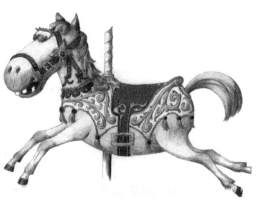

DID YOU SEE?

At the fairground, there's a little notice in front of the Hot Dog stand that says 'Hot Dogs, and Cats and Burgers'. It's an affectionate nod towards DreamWorks co-founder Jeffrey Katzenberg.

The Church

As with everything in Wallace and Gromit's world, the first consideration was to meet the overall look of 'typical, but slightly exaggerated cartoon characteristics'. Both Nick Park and Steve Box considered that market town parish church characteristics were more important than 'typical northern town' qualities. "So between us," production designer Phil Lewis explains, "the Wallace and Gromit 'cartoon' characteristics of an aisled nave with the chancel at the east end and a tower at the west end was decided upon."

Next, using the available storyboards of the three sequences featuring the church — the Vicar being attacked in the church, the church hall meeting, and the vegetable hospital (which was later dropped) — simple sketches were created, and a number of cardboard models at various scales (1:10, 1:5 and 1:1) were made using stand-in puppets. These cardboard mockups were examined using a director's viewfinder, checking the composition and framing on various lenses. They were also viewed using a tiny video camera.

"Having established pleasing composition and the basic needs of story telling, and therefore the accommodation of crowd scenes, harvest festival displays etc, the overall width, depth and height could be fixed," Phil Lewis notes. The church was then divided into manageable sections to come apart and go back together in as many configurations as possible, to accommodate camera positions, animator access and lighting requirements. The decision was taken to have eighteen floor sections, fifteen wall sections, six arcade sections and ten roof sections. The joins were created where possible where architectural detail made for easier set dressing.

The preparation of drawings for the set builders and model makers could now begin. "Having always had an interest in Medieval buildings, of which churches are the most numerous, I found the logical way to approach the visual structure and detail was to build in its history," Phil says. "To do this, in my mind I pictured the church having its roots in a simple twelfth century nave, with transepts, tower over the crossing, and the altar in the sanctuary, in a cruciform shape. Sometime in the thirteenth century, the sanctuary would have gone, and been replaced with the chancel.

"Another 150 years would pass and the nave would have its aisles (north and south) added, so therefore columns would arrive, along with more stained glass. In the fifteenth or sixteenth century, the tower over the crossing would go, and a new west tower added. Then, after the upheaval of the Reformation and a bit of Victorian messing about, we find, with more than a little artistic licence, the church we see in the film.

"It was therefore possible to use a wide range of interesting church architectural elements. So, with a liberal splash of artistic licence, I could position fine details where they were most likely to be seen."

Once the drawings were completed, and examples and photo references for colour and texture were supplied, the build was overseen in the workshops and then taken on to the studio floor.

Opposite: A couple of the intricately designed stained glass windows.

Below: Maria Hopkinson-Hassell and Dug Calder animate the townsfolk in the church.

"I like doing churches. It's a hobby of mine looking at churches, so I didn't find it particularly difficult. It is a mix, like real churches are: a mix of styles and a mix of periods. It looks so quaint because it is pretty much in my opinion typical, as much as it can be."

Phil Lewis - Production designer

St · NORM

St · STAN

The Woods

The prizes for both the spookiest and the largest set in the movie has to go to the woods outside the town, the same woods where Gromit first sees Wallace turning into the Were-rabbit. "The woods set was probably thirty to forty foot long and twenty foot wide at its widest point," senior set dresser Andy Brown recalls. "The basic sets would arrive from Cod Steaks, the set building company. We would then put in extra tracks and bed in trees and roots. The canopy of the forest was made from squares of chicken wire which we would loop leaves into. It was a tricky operation — all the branches of the trees were made of wire as well, so when we were trying to climb through them, it was like wrestling kittens."

Fortunately the full woodland set was only seen a handful of times. "There's probably only about three establishing shots," says Andy. "The close-ups look beautiful, but all around them is absolute chaos. Trees have been snapped and things have been spilt all over the set, but it's so big you don't have to worry about that."

The woodland scenes were the trickiest ones to shoot in the entire film. Not only did they frequently involve a model covered in fur, but the directors wanted them to be made more mysterious with drifting fog, something that never does the same thing twice in the real world.

"This film has got to have fog, to get that typical Gothic Hammer horror feel," says David Alex-Riddett, the film's director of photography, along with Tristan Oliver. "But how the hell do you do fog? It's like smoke and fire when you're animating. So we thought we'd bite the bullet — we'd do it for real this time, we'd somehow devise a way of having these animated characters move around a live-action material."

In the end, the solution involved a combination of lighting, photographic technique and sophisticated computer technology (courtesy of an external company called The Moving Picture Company).

"We would shoot a scene completely clean, without the fog or anything," explains David Alex-Riddett. "We'd just try to get the atmosphere right with the lighting. We would shoot that as an empty scene with a camera move, then shoot again with the characters walking through the scene but every time we took a frame, we'd take a shot of the characters, and we'd then take another shot of them with an illuminated green card behind them, so every position they were in, there was also a silhouette version of it. That would enable MPC to take the characters *out* of the scene and put them into what was later a fog filled scene, and then put a bit of fog over it as well to blend them in."

"The live action smoke stuff does work really well," says production designer Phil Lewis, "and it mixes well with Nick's opinion of the kind of films he makes, which he describes as being comedy thrillers."

"I did all the shots in the woods with the Were-rabbit lifting his log up and chucking it, which was all against green screen. I would shoot what we call a 'beauty frame' and then put in a green screen board, and take a frame. That gives you a matte of the model so they can combine the background plate and fog with the puppet. But when you get the rushes back, everything's at half speed because you've got green flashes every other frame, so everything is moving in slow motion! I'm looking at the Were-rabbit's fur and can't tell if it's 'boiling' or not. It's great when it finally comes back [from post-production] and it's got this live action fog floating around."

Ian Whitlock - Key animator

"All the forest scenes were shrouded in fog. This meant the sets were covered in dry ice and shot as live action beauty plates against green screen. This was very handy because it meant you could do the forest quite quickly; you could throw leaves and twigs down because it didn't matter that they weren't locked off and steady. Usually with a set you have to make sure that everything is rigid."

Andy Brown - Senior set dresser

Opposite: Merlin Crossingham (second unit director) animates the van disappearing down the track in the woods.

Below: Tristan Oliver (director of photography) tests lighting and fog.

Setpiece Three: "The Beast Within"

A key scene in the movie occurs when Victor confronts the Vicar, and the truth about the Were-rabbit — and how to defeat it — is revealed. It's just a conversation, there are few jokes and even less action, but it moves the plot along and ratchets the tension up several notches. The scene's genesis went back to the time that directors Nick Park and Steve Box spent watching old horror films when they were planning the movie.

"The character of the Vicar came from *The Curse of the Werewolf*, the Hammer film with Oliver Reed," says Steve. "There's a vicar in that. He doesn't look like our vicar, but Nick and I laughed and laughed when watching that film. The film's hero goes to the vicar for supernatural knowledge, and we just couldn't understand it: why do vicars have this amazing knowledge of the paranormal? When you watch it you accept it, but if you think about it, it's absolutely crazy. And so we really wanted that kind of vicar in it, that mad logic."

As film editor Gregory Perler points out, the scene also served to allow the audience to catch their breath after a particularly fast-moving action sequence. "We've just had an exciting time prior with the Were-rabbit transformation," Gregory says, "and I didn't mind slowing things down a bit and taking it all in, especially for the Vicar pontificating."

The scene was built up in the same way as any other. Initial storyboard sketches of particular shots — close-ups of Victor or the Vicar, shots of them together, cut-aways to props — were pinned on a wall and moved around until the entire sequence was mapped out. The storyboards were then put onto film (using an editing machine and computer edit machine) and the soundtrack was added on, for timing purposes (with the occasional eye movement or change of expression added to the storyboards to provide some variety). This is known as an 'animatic' sequence or story reel.

"It was well storyboarded, but it never had any atmosphere," laments Gregory Perler. "Whenever you have a scene that is visually dark, it's hard with white sketch paper and black lines to get any sense of mood, and the whole last third of the movie takes place in the dark. There are lots of other night scenes that lead up to it that are incredibly atmospheric and you just don't get it at all in the storyboards."

The scene's importance is shown by the care that was taken to get it right. "I know Steve Box was particularly obsessive about picking the dialogue takes," says Gregory. "He would select some takes with Angharad Owen, the editor, and cut them in, then he would change a few and we would think 'we're done', but then we'd have to go back and change a line."

Left: Director of photography
David Alex-Riddett checks
lighting for a still.

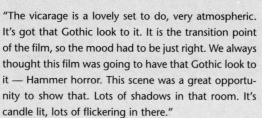

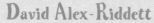

Left: The Vicar's collection of arcane material – from garlic to Shankara stones.

"The vicarage is a lovely set to do, very atmospheric. It's got that Gothic look to it. It is the transition point of the film, so the mood had to be just right. We always thought this film was going to have that Gothic look to it — Hammer horror. This scene was a great opportunity to show that. Lots of shadows in that room. It's candle lit, lots of flickering in there."

David Alex-Riddett
- Director of photography

"I made the books. I'd done book binding when I was at college. [Graphic designer] Gavin Lines did the illustrations in the middle, which were beautiful. I went to a book binding place and got them to just sew the leaves together. I made two versions that are identical, and hopefully you can't tell the difference. The small one is probably about two inches tall and the bigger one is probably six inches, something like that, because they're working at different scales."

Jane Kite - Prop maker supervisor

The Inventions:
The Anti-pesto Van

They used a motorcycle-sidecar combination in *A Close Shave*, and were seen in a Renault Kangoo in a more recent TV advert, but in *The Curse of the Were-rabbit* Wallace and Gromit appear to have finally found their ideal means of conveyance — a 1950s-vintage Austin A35 van.

"My brother used to have one, and I've always liked those vans," Nick Park reveals. "If there was a style of car in Wallace and Gromit's world, it would be that one."

Although Wallace and Gromit have never actually been seen driving one before, this isn't the first time that the A35 appears in their adventures.

"That van actually appears in *The Wrong Trousers*," Nick admits. "We made the whole thing, but sometimes used just the back of it, or just the front, so it could double up as two cars. You can see it when the penguin's walking past the café. I never actually thought Wallace and Gromit would have one."

Replicating the van in all its glory but at a fraction of its size was a task which fell to independent model maker John Wright (who also provided internal metal skeletons for the many characters in the film).

"The actual van body was cast in a polyurethane resin," he says, "which was then primed and painted. Other parts — all the metalwork like the bumpers, door handles and wheel hubs — we cast in brass which we then plated so it has a very real look. Not like spraying with silver paint: that looks a bit rubbish. We did all the rust and corrosion and dents on the master panel, which means all the rust patches are all identical on each duplicate van, and we then painted the duplicates with rust colours."

Then they had to make it move like a real A35. "Early on we took out a real A35 van and tried skidding it around corners," reveals David Alex-Riddett, director of photography, "photographing it and seeing what happened." Using the results of their tests, Aardman's animators set to work giving the A35 weight and momentum, making it rock on its suspension and corner like a real van. And they succeeded so well the van is almost a character in its own right.

Above: Matt Perry, art director, compares the Anti-pesto van to its life-size replica.

Opposite above: Pascual Pérez Porcar animates Gromit in the van.

Opposite centre: Supervising animator Loyd Price poses Gromit.

Opposite below: Director of photography David Alex-Riddett shoots the van.

The sounds made by the van were recorded from an actual A35 van, borrowed specifically for the occasion. The Austin A35 van was produced between 1956 and 1959. It had an engine capacity of 948cc, a top speed of 75mph and a petrol consumption of around forty-two miles per gallon (although it probably won't achieve that with Wallace at the wheel).

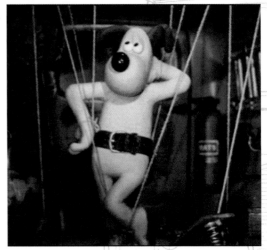

"There was a large-scale version, which had the full-scale puppets in for the close-up work, and then there was a smaller one, scaled to the sets, with the smaller puppets in, and then there were some specials — one with stabilisers, and others with various gadgets like the auto-start handle coming out."

"The worst part was it was a pristine model the first time, and then Nick said, 'Wallace is a bit of a rubbish driver, so we need a few dents in there.' We took it back and put some dents in. It took about four attempts before Nick was happy with it. It was a case of, 'Go back, think about how much you want to dent it, and double it.' We couldn't dent it enough."

"Everything is rounded off and slightly inflated. It just gives it that 'Wallace and Gromit' look. It's not like a scale model: it has its own look and feel to it."

"The van actually has stop motion suspension, operated by the animator. By operating hidden screws, it actually jacks the body to the left or right, or front and back. You can get a roll going with it. It's the animator that gives it that floaty suspension feeling."

John Wright - Independent model maker,
John Wright Modelmaking

Bun-vac 6000

Wallace's Bun-vac 6000 is perhaps his greatest invention to date. The movable apparatus can be installed either in the cellar of 62 West Wallaby Street, or within the confines of Wallace's beloved A35 van.

It operates on the simple principle of suction. Place the nozzle in the rabbit hole, switch on, and bunnies are dragged away from their lettuce-guzzling antics and pulled along the burrows towards the machine where they are held in a vortex within the glass storage jar. As Wallace proudly informs Lady Tottington, it works at 125 'r.p.m.' — that's 'rabbits per minute'. It's even powerful enough to pull a full grown man into the ground.

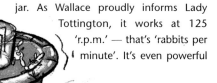

To make the Bun-vac fit within Wallace and Gromit's world, production designer Phil Lewis and his team followed the usual formula of removing it slightly from the contemporary world. Then, once a design had been agreed with the directors, the blueprints were sent outside Aardman to John Wright's model making company. "It had been very thoroughly designed," John recalls. "We virtually were given plans to make that from, but again we had to work out a way to do it. It was quite complicated, because there's so much glass, and there were all these rabbits going to be inside."

According to the script, 'Hutch bursts out into the glass storage jar of the Bun-vac 6000. He floats rapturously around in zero gravity.' But how could that be achieved? Although the rabbits were eventually realised using computer generated imagery, the Bun-vac was designed so that the rabbits could be animated traditionally. "The animator had to be able to get inside there and animate them," John explains, "so the Bun-vac came apart. There were sliding panels that came apart and sections that you could lift off."

The 'glass' panels weren't in fact made from glass. "We used Perspex," John says. "They did quite a few tests with glass, Perspex and other materials, and in the end we used an extruded Perspex tube. That was a bit snappy when it was being cut on a circular saw, a little bit tricky to do. It turned out that it wasn't the most perfect material because it has ripples in it, but when they did the test, Nick really liked it."

Tests were carried out to see if it would be possible to animate the rabbits traditionally. "We had these twelve rabbits on sticks, but we couldn't achieve that smoothness of rotation which is the perfect thing for CGI," Steve Box continues. "I'd done some CGI work on a Wallace and Gromit commercial for Japan, and I've used CGI for backgrounds. We gave the CGI guys an asteroid made out of Plasticine, they copied it and you couldn't tell the difference."

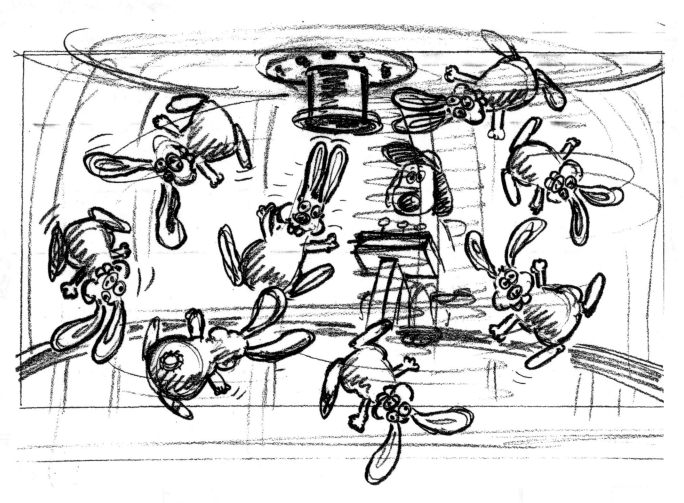

"Nick had the basic idea, and then we had to work out what it does. That led to sorting out the sizes that were necessary. We worked those out, and mocked them up. Nick said that it was loosely like a cylinder vacuum cleaner, but it was never going to be exactly like one except that it's got a glass cylinder. It had to look far more like something from the 1950s than that. It had to be much more robust-looking than a vacuum cleaner. We explored other areas of design to see how panels were riveted then, and how they were bent and made. We tend to do quite a lot of research into things like that — we look at a lot of references."

Phil Lewis - Production designer

Above: Nick Park's concept of bunnies in the Bun-vac's vortex.

Opposite: Key animator Ian Whitlock adjusts the bunnies' eyeline.

"We have a constant battle with gravity. So I was incredibly in favour of doing the bunny CGI before anybody else was. Everybody else was absolutely committed to doing them in Plasticine. But that would be impossible for the vision that Nick and I had of them, swirling around in zero gravity. If you think of a character doing that, it's rotating on every single axis. They would have to be rigged, and you could still then only spin them on one axis — you wouldn't be able to spin them on every axis. Plus there are loads of them — we wanted the Bun-vac to be full."

Steve Box - Director

"They sent these little Plasticine bunnies on an armature which we scanned onto the computer to get their shape. We also used them as a reference for the Plasticine material, not only in terms of colour, but also for the subtleties of the surface texture. We've got to make sure our CG stuff has exactly the same texture as the real stuff — the bumpiness of the surface, the thumb prints, the various imperfections, little tiny cracks. All of those have got to be mimicked."

"We're very aware that in the film there are a lot of Plasticine bunnies as well as the CG ones, and in some cases, you cut from one shot that has got real bunnies in to our shots with the same bunnies created in CG. We were utterly delighted to hear second hand that some animators and even one of the directors of photography were looking at one of our shots and querying whether it was a CG one or a real one."

Paddy Eason - VFX supervisor,
The Moving Picture Company

"We had to make the effect of that light on the walls and inside the Bun-vac. We built a lot of lights into the floor of the Bun-vac: it's got a perforated steel floor and we had lights underneath, and lights hidden in the top of it. After every shot we'd do a background plate using thin bars of light that we projected onto the walls and animated those up as if the rings were throwing light onto the wall."

Tristan Oliver - Director of photography

The Mind-Manipulation-O-Matic

"If I must change me ways, at least let me do it my way — with technology," Wallace tells Gromit, and it's hardly surprising that with his master's track record, Gromit looks extremely worried when Wallace not only tries to use his new invention to cure himself of his cheese habit but also tries to brainwash the rabbits and achieve rabbit rehabilitation.

Designed and built in a similar way to the Bun-vac, with which it operates in tandem, the Mind-Manipulation-O-Matic is the cause of the Curse of the Were-rabbit. "One thing we realised early on was that the Were-rabbit had to be Wallace," director Steve Box explains. "It couldn't be anybody else. So we had to find a way for him to become a were-rabbit."

In the traditional werewolf film, the innocent victim is turned after they are bitten by another werewolf, and can only be released from their affliction if they are shot by a silver bullet. "It's a really curious death," Steve notes. "The silver bullet releases their soul. But we couldn't kill Wallace, so we concocted all these crazy ideas of how he could get infected."

The writers went through various different notions. "We didn't want to get into serums or injections," Steve recalls, "so we realised really that he couldn't get bitten or scratched." One idea that was discarded involved Wallace having an accident in the rabbit pen at West Wallaby Street when it was full of bunnies. "He had to feed them, and fell in, but it was just horrible," Steve says.

"Eventually the idea was that Wallace was trying to brainwash the rabbits, and it backfired," Steve continues. "Somehow bunny neurones got muddled up along with the DNA, and the reversal would just be to do it back the other way again. It took a long time to sort that out!"

One horror film tribute comes from the lunar panels with which Wallace powers the Mind-Manipulation-O-Matic. Traditionally, the appearance of the full moon heralds the beginning of the transformation from man into werewolf, and the same thing happens here. Although quite why he thinks that 'lunar power' will enhance the mind-waves, only Wallace knows...

Right: A Nick Park sketch of Gromit operating the Mind-Manipulation-O-Matic.

Opposite: Shooting stills for the Mind-Manipulation-O-Matic sequence.

DID YOU SEE?

While he waits for the Mind-Manipulation-O-Matic to do its work, Wallace is reading the northern equivalent to *Hello* magazine — *Ay-Up!*

"For the mind-waves we were given a couple of reference points — the rings of ener-gy that surround the lady robot in *Metropolis* and smoke rings. We ordered a couple of toy smoke ring guns off the internet and played around with them until we had a good feel for how real smoke rings work. Our challenge was to make mind-waves that were ethereal and strange, but also fitted well into the very physical Wallace and Gromit universe."

Paddy Eason - VFX supervisor, The Moving Picture Company

"To make the mind-waves we first animated giant donut shapes that acted as the base for the effect. These donuts were made to 'spring', 'wobble' and 'roll' and let us establish the character of the mind-wave's movement. Then using three-dimensional blurring techniques the donuts were made into gaseous volumes and coloured in distinctive 'vegetable' colours. Extra dynamic effects where added giv-ing the mind-waves stringy and sparkly elements, which when rendered with the bunny rabbits and the gaseous cores produced the final mind-waves."

Ben Toogood - CG lighting artist

Domestic Inventions

Wallace is probably the most visionary inventor that Great Britain has ever produced. From the rocket to the moon that was the centrepiece of *A Grand Day Out* to the Bun-vac and Mind-Manipulation-O-Matic that cause so much trouble in *The Curse of the Were-rabbit*, his fertile imagination can devise ways of dealing with any conceivable problem. Though Wallace's efforts to simplify life sometimes have the opposite effect…

Want to get up with less effort in the morning? Easy with the cracking contraptions that Wallace has installed in his bedroom, all controlled by Get-U-Up wall levers, handily located in the kitchen so Gromit can operate them while preparing breakfast.

Don't want to waste all that time pulling on clothes, and bending down to put your shoes on? No trouble,

with the wonderful dressing machine that fits within the dining room of West Wallaby Street.

There's even a hidden compartment in the bookcase for Wallace to hide his secret cheese stash in case of emergencies — like Gromit putting him on a diet.

And if all that labour-saving — and cheese consumption — *does* lead to some 'middle-aged spread', there's always the assistance lever, which operates a giant mallet installed in Wallace's bedroom wardrobe…

However, although Wallace's inventions are scattered throughout *The Curse of the Were-rabbit*, there aren't as many of them as you might expect considering Wallace and Gromit have recently been demonstrating their *Cracking Contraptions*.

"Partly that's the way things have gone, out of necessity," director Nick Park says. "We didn't sit down and decide not to put so many inventions in."

Not that Nick wouldn't have liked to have had more inventions in the film, but with a running time of eighty minutes, and a plot to unfold, something had to give. "The problem is on something the size of this film, you've got to follow where the story takes you," he says, "and so, as Oscar Wilde said, you've got to 'murder your own darlings'. You feel a bit like a mass murderer, committing genocide every day!"

Below and opposite: Nick Park drawings of Gromit helping Wallace get up in the morning.

"The design of the inventions are storyboard-led, script-led and are essentially Nick's. They are integral to the story and to Wallace and Gromit's world, so Nick normally has a pretty clear idea of what there is in his mind, but he seldom gets it past a few sketches, and a few pencil lines. The storyboard artists normally run with what he gives them, and they don't normally much vary from that."

"It's mostly [art director] Matt Perry who pursues and keeps on developing [Nick's] ideas. He brings them on, gives them shape and form, substance and thickness — all the other things that are needed — and then goes on to resolve the way that they work."

Phil Lewis - Production designer

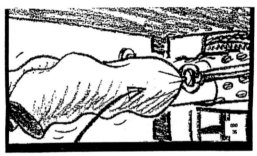

 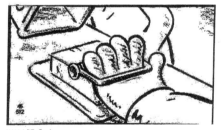 

Above top: Wallace's secret cheese compartment in the bookcase.

Above: Gromit turns the tables with a device to ensure Wallace stays on his diet.

Opposite: Another of Wallace's inventions, this time to help get dressed at the breakfast table.

Among the several books in Wallace's library is *Brie Encounter*, which might be related to David Lean's 1945 film (scripted by Noel Coward) *Brief Encounter*.

Anti-pesto Inventions

Gone are the days when pest controllers used a stick and a large bag to catch their prey. In the high-tech world of Wallace and Gromit, every possible item that they might need to stop the pesky varmints in their tracks has been thought of, visualised and made for use. In the back of the A35 van, in addition to space for the Bun-vac when it's needed, there are racks of tools which our heroes can grab at a moment's notice.

All of these in reality derive from the fertile imagination of the directors, Nick Park and Steve Box, and considerable discussion goes on throughout the manufacture process to ensure that everything is keeping to their vision. The models are shown to the directors, who indicate, either verbally or with little line drawings, any changes that they might want. They then request functioning props of the ones that they like. The whole process is extremely quick. "I showed one item to Nick yesterday, and it's being filmed on set today," prop maker supervisor Jane Kite points out.

Left: Second unit director Merlin Crossingham animates Wallace at Tottington Hall.

Vicar: "Bless you Anti-pesto! With you out there protecting our veg, the most important event of the year is safe!"

"A lot of those things are largely in Nick or Steve's mind, depending on who is directing the sequence, but usually Nick has got some close idea. Because they are an area of the production where a puppet is coming into immediate contact with animatable props, the directors tend to have more say, and they're made in-house. We tend not to draw them up and send them off to be made and then bring them in. We do send them away to make up loads of variations of the originals, but because so much is required of the props, we tend to keep them in-house."

Phil Lewis - Production designer

Above: Merlin Crossingham animates Wallace catching a rabbit.

Opposite: The kettle invention that starts the Anti-pesto launch sequence.

"There are loads of those pest-getting-rid-of tools in the inside of the van. I go to a meeting with the directors, and see exactly what is required. Then I go and get some reference material, and make a few little cut-outs, so that the characters can hold them. From that, we can then work out the scale — everything in Wallace and Gromit's world is just a teeny bit bigger and a teeny bit chunkier than it would be in the real world, but it's got the essential quality of the object, which we have to get right."

Jane Kite - Prop maker supervisor

This page: Various stages of Gromit operating the Lady Were-rabbit.

DID YOU SEE?

Gromit uses a 'mutt', rather than 'mute', button to quiet the sound on the radio in his Austin A35 van. The tune he is listening to, by the way, is 'Bright Eyes' — Mike Batt's theme song from the 1978 film about a colony of rabbits, *Watership Down*.

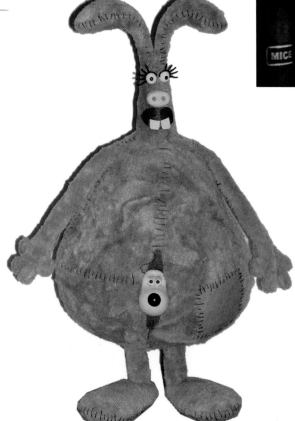

Setpiece Four:
The Finale

J ust five short months before the release date, decisions were still being taken as to the way the film was going to end. Heroes had to be triumphant, of course, and villains had to get their comeuppance, but the previous shorts had set a bar sufficiently high that the production team were finding it a challenge to get over.

"Once the button is pressed on story reel development," explains development executive Mike Cooper, "you have a situation where the script is still being written but sequences are being storyboarded, then shooting starts to kick in, and all those three processes are going on at the same time."

The fight up on the roof of Tottington Hall remained constant through many versions of the film — dating back to early ideas, such as Victor Quartermaine actually being Tristram Tottington, Lady Tottington's son — but the details kept changing.

"At one point," says director Steve Box, "I remember that Gromit, near the end of the film, was trying to get up to the rooftops and he had this fight with Tristram Tottington in Tristram's old nursery. They had this big fight with toys. The idea was that no matter

what this villain did, everything conspired to make him feel like a child."

One thing that remained constant through all versions was Wallace's transition from Were-rabbit back to inventor again. Easy enough to achieve with real actors and make-up, it proved to be trickier with Plasticine.

"I did the reverse transformation: Were-rabbit into Wallace," says second unit director Merlin Crossingham. "It's going to be a faded effect, through the different stages, and then with Gromit wafting Stinky Bishop cheese under Wallace's nose and Wallace coming round going "Cheese!" With that particular shot, the camera was so close to Wallace that I couldn't actually get in to sculpt him. I had to get the rigging department to make a rig so I could physically pick him up and take him off the set, sculpt him and then put him back. Registering him was a real problem, in that I had to take him off set about a dozen times. If we take a puppet off the set and then bring it back, it has to register to exactly the same position that it was when we took it off, otherwise when it's played back on film, you get a jittery twitching which is completely unacceptable, because it gives away any form of solidity."

Vicar: "Ah, Mr Growbag! I have a hunch
this'll be a night to remember!"

Mr Growbag: "I just have a hunch."

"Today, Nick pitched a new gag: when Victor has the beast cornered on the roof of Tottington Hall, and it's moving to the balustrade and debris falls down, PC Mac is going to say, 'Beware — large rabbit dropping!' That's being storyboarded now and cut in."

Gregory Perler - Film editor
(six months before the release date)

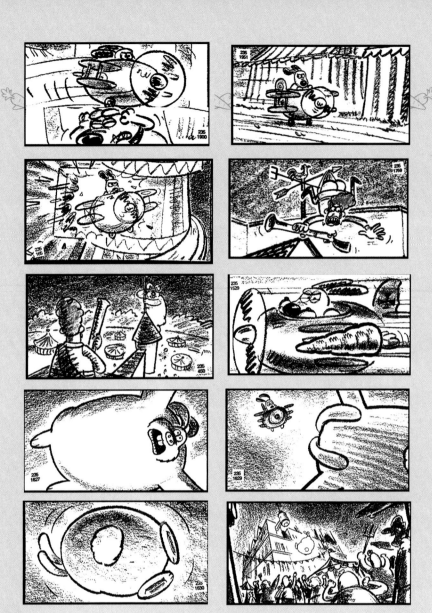

Below: Philip and Gromit in a 'dogfight', as conceived by Steve Box.

"Nick knows what gags are working and they find things out from the reel and the feedback they get. At the moment we're working on PC Mac to get him back into the action. There was a gag of him swallowing his loudhailer — he's hit by the beast and he swallows his loudhailer, and he speaks with this huge megaphone voice for the rest of the film. It was in, then it was out..."

Michael Salter - Senior storyboard artist

"I had to get a piece [of the Stinking Bishop cheese] to copy for the sequence where Gromit revives Wallace. It's made in Dorset. There was a delicatessen in Thornbury, so I just had to ring them and try and get hold of it. I had so many complaints! In fact I got really powerful and chased people around with it after a while. It smells like rotting vegetables. I imagine it's like a gangrenous leg or something!"

Jane Kite - Prop maker supervisor

Pulling it All Together

In early April, when the interviews for this book were carried out, there were thirty different units operating at Aardman Features in Bristol, all working on various facets of the movie — adding a new gag to existing footage here, shooting all new material for the ending there. In his studio in London, composer Julian Nott was hard at work on the score for the film. In their offices in Soho, Central London, Paddy Eason and the crew at The Moving Picture Company were rendering the computer generated sequences of the rabbits in the Bun-vac, as well as working on other aspects of post-production. In a studio elsewhere in London, members of the voice cast were limbering up to record pick-up lines. Five thou-

sand miles away in California, DreamWorks executives were pondering the marketing for the movie in conjunction with the film's producers and Aardman's own marketing department.

So how did it all come together to create one eighty or so minute movie a mere twenty weeks later? The answer is with a great deal of careful planning. From the moment that directors Nick Park and Steve Box first worked on the story ideas, everyone's efforts were focussed on achieving that end result, with the film's shape becoming increasingly clear as time went on.

Like any film, *The Curse of the Were-rabbit* went through various versions. "In its way," explains editor Gregory Perler, "the script is an incarnation. The story-

board artists work on it, and that's another incarnation, we get what they do [and fine tune or rearrange it], which is yet another incarnation, and then it's animated."

All of those versions can feel like totally different stories, as composer Julian Nott notes. Unusually, Julian, who has written the music for all of Wallace and Gromit's adventures to date, was brought in at the very early stages. "I wrote some score for the storyboards," he recalls. "The mood of the film has changed from the storyboard to the actual animation an awful lot, so the music I wrote for the storyboards inevitably felt wrong later on."

The storyboards are photographed and run together in a 'show reel', and as each piece of film is animated and passed by the directors, the editors replace the storyboards with the proper footage. "That's what Dave [McCormick] and I love about coming in in the morning," Gregory Perler says. "What new shots came in today that are waiting for us so we can take out the story sketch and put them in here?"

The editors add sound effects and music. "When Nick views a piece of animation initially, he sees it on film, but only has a synch track of the voice," editor David McCormick explains. "Then we put it into the AVID machine, and when he sees it cut in with music and effects, it sometimes alters how he sees the image."

Seeing the footage in context allows the directors, as well as the producers and the studio, to judge whether a sequence works or not. "As animation starts to come in and the scene plays in a gap-toothed way, we watch it in context, and we get feedback from the studio that they 'understand it but we're not feeling it — maybe we could see Gromit see this activity happen and put two and two together in his mind?'" Gregory says.

At this point, new material can be shot if required, sometimes against green screen so that it can be skilfully inserted into the existing material when a photographic plate of the set is added in the background. This is part of the compositing work that The Moving Picture Company has been doing for the film, making everything shot over the long period appear part of one unified world.

"We've been involved for about two years now, alongside the main shoot," VFX supervisor Paddy Eason says. "We've done the general compositing, where the animators have chosen to shoot in different passes, and a lot of effects animation — the stuff they find harder to do with clay. That includes adding things like rain, flying sawdust, sparks, smoke — all those kind of slightly ethereal things."

Whether it's a prop for Wallace to hold, or a computer generated effect, everything must have what director Steve Box describes as a "more chunky" look than it would have in the real world. "We have to take their visual lead and work out what the rules are," Paddy says. "To fit into this world of 'chunky' movements, we have to throw away the rulebook of proper physics, and do this weird stylised thing. Which is very good fun! You occasionally come across weird quirks where something is really quite difficult to do on software that is designed to produce photo quality real-life action, and you have to come up with workarounds to give things the gnarliness they need to have in the Wallace and Gromit world."

Once the film has been edited together, MPC produce the final negative. "We're doing the colour grading and conforming," Paddy explains, "and putting everything together according to the edit, ready for the labs to take over and make the thousands of prints that are required."

While MPC work on the visuals, the sound will be mixed, with all the various unusual sound effects that are needed added to the dialogue, and Julian Nott's score. The final version of the music is written as the picture nears completion, and will be recorded by a

ninety-piece orchestra. All aspects of the film have to be finely balanced. "The horror and the comedy are totally intertwined," Julian notes. "You don't want the jokes to be wiped out. Audiences tend to laugh better if they've had a signal to say 'this is funny' somewhere."

Public awareness of the movie is important. The preview at the Cannes Film Festival was well received, and audiences enjoyed the teaser trailer. Footage was shown to test audiences as far afield as Wimbledon and Utah. For overseas audiences, *The Curse of the Were-rabbit* might be their first encounter with Wallace and Gromit, and it was important to judge what would entice them to come to the cinema. "DreamWorks wanted to find the most virgin territory they could," producer David Sproxton says of the Utah screening. "There was something like thirty-six or thirty-eight percent awareness of Wallace and Gromit beforehand, which was amazing. But imagine people seeing the characters for the first time…"

And if everyone at Aardman has anything to do with it, it won't be the last. "I think Nick has realised the potential of Wallace and Gromit," David Sproxton says, "and what more he can do with them…"

Above: Andrew Ward, first assistant editor.

Opposite: Steve Box on set.

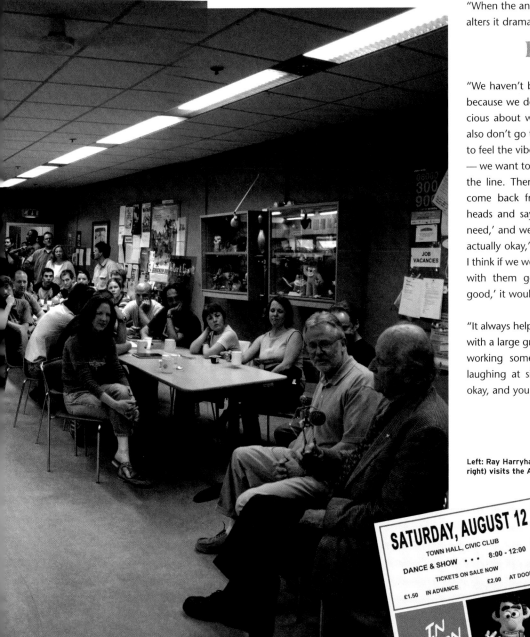

"When the animation comes in from the storyboard, it alters it dramatically. Suddenly, it's a living thing."

David McCormick - Film editor

"We haven't been down on the set at all on purpose because we don't want to see it, and then get as precious about what's been filmed as anybody else. We also don't go to the recording sessions. We don't want to feel the vibe in the room with *Ralph Fiennes* doing it — we want to know what we've got from *Victor* saying the line. There are lots of times when the directors come back from a recording session rubbing their heads and saying, 'I don't know if we got what we need,' and we'll cut it together and they'll say, 'That's actually okay,' but we weren't there, part of that vibe. I think if we were and had to take a two hour trip home with them going, 'Hmmm don't think it went so good,' it would probably colour what we do."

"It always helps to take it out of a vacuum and watch it with a large group of people. Things you thought were working sometimes don't, and things you stopped laughing at six months ago, you realise are actually okay, and you have lost your objectivity about it."

Gregory Perler - Film editor

Left: Ray Harryhausen (far right) visits the Aardman studio.

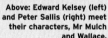
Above: Edward Kelsey (left) and Peter Sallis (right) meet their characters, Mr Mulch and Wallace.

"The difficulty I have with all of this is balancing expressing the excitement which comes from playing with the horror genre with not killing the jokes by doing so."

"There's a lot of music, but there's less for *The Curse of the Were-rabbit* than in some Hollywood animations which are quite literally scored from beginning to end. You do have a little bit of respite now and again. You need to give your ears a rest — it can get very tiring to have loud music all the time, and fifteen or even thirty seconds with no music is often very effective."

"Horror music didn't really work very well with the comedy of the film. It was a little bit too oppressive. It seemed more conventional to use a more up-to-date style of film music. Some horror music is very harsh. The film was originally temped with some of the score from *The Omen* and things like that, and it did seem to give the film a slightly nasty edge. Wallace and Gromit want to be extremely warm and cuddly, so it didn't seem right."

"People associate mainly very loud, dissonant music with horror, but they're also used to the idea of nursery rhymes and horror waltzes, even though they're not consciously aware that they are often used. I didn't feel I could use the dissonant style because of the comedy."

Julian Nott - Composer

Above: Nick Park presents the film at Cannes with producers David Sproxton and Peter Lord, and DreamWorks co-founder Jeffrey Katzenberg.

"Every single frame of the movie is being scanned digitally, treated in some manner, whether it's adding digital bunnies, or sweetening the colour."

Paddy Eason - VFX supervisor, The Moving Picture Company

"Usually films take about six weeks to edit. I've actually been on this film for two and a half years. That's a lifetime."

David McCormick - Film editor

"I always thought things would be improved or honed down — jokes might need to be added — but I wasn't prepared for the amount. It's quite difficult to cope with, especially when you have thirty animators shooting. It's like this huge relentless machine kicks into motion. But at the same time producers and financiers are encouraging you to keep changing things."

Steve Box - Director

DID YOU SEE?

According to director Steve Box, the penguin from *The Wrong Trousers* appears in *The Curse of the Were-rabbit*. "I'm not going to tell you where," he says. "All I can say is he's really easy to spot, if you know where to look. He's actually on screen for a good seven or eight seconds."

FROM THE CREATORS OF CHICKEN RUN

Master.

Mind.

Wallace & Gromit
THE CURSE OF THE WERE-RABBIT

Coming Soon.

www.wallaceandgromitmovie.co.uk

FROM THE CREATORS OF **CHICKEN RUN**

Wallace & Gromit

THE CURSE OF THE WERE-RABBIT

COMING SOON TO CINEMAS

www.wallaceandgromitmovie.co.uk

Aardman

united international pictures

DREAMWORKS
ANIMATION SKG

Watch the movie and read the books!

Join your favorite duo, Wallace & Gromit, as they solve the Curse of the Were-rabbit—and save the day!

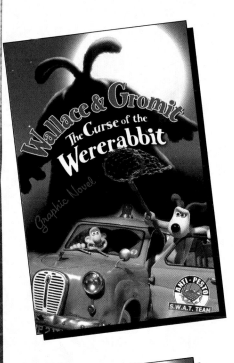

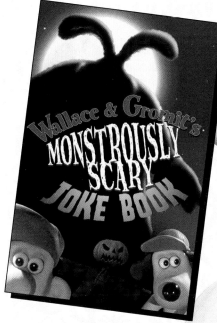

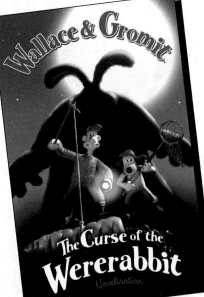

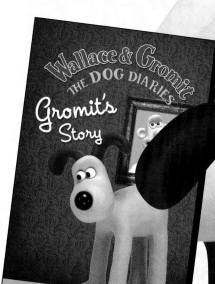

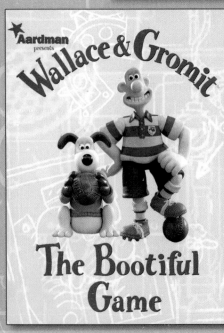